By Heart

By Heart

REFLECTIONS OF A RUST BELT BARD

Philip Brady

1/10/16

To Vanessa O'Connor
With admiration +
hopes for your work at
a [illegible]

THE UNIVERSITY OF TENNESSEE PRESS / KNOXVILLE

FIRST EDITION.

This book is printed on acid-free paper.

Library of Congress Cataloging-in-Publication Data

Brady, Philip, 1955–
By heart: reflections of a rust belt bard / Philip Brady. — 1st ed.
    p. cm.
Includes bibliographical references.
ISBN-13: 978-1-57233-632-2 (acid-free paper)
ISBN-10: 1-57233-632-3
 1. Brady, Philip, 1955–
 2. Poetics.
 I. Title.

PS3552.R2437Z46 2008
813'.54—dc22

2008010461

Contents

Acknowledgments

I AM GRATEFUL to the editors of the following journals and anthologies, in which some of these essays first appeared: *College English*, "Teaching Tu Fu on the Night Shift"; *The Connecticut Review*, "Books of Sand: A Review of Unpublished Manuscripts, One a Conceit of Its Author" and "Teaching Like My Fathers"; *Green Mountains Review*, "My Dinner with Joe"; *New Myths/Mss*, "Wiretap" (poem); *Provincetown Arts*, "Letter to Ireland" and "This Is Heyen Speaking"; *The Drunken Boat*, "By Heart: Curriculum for a Bardic School"; *Ohio Writer*, "Ginsberg in Ballydehob"; *Ordering the Storm* (Cleveland State University Press), "The Shapes a Bright Container Can Contain"; *Pennsylvania English*, "Entangled Music"; *The Radical Teacher*, "The Scholar in the Hayfield"; *September 11, 2001: American Writers Respond* (Etruscan Press), "Letter to Bill Heyen"; *Thought and Action*, "Tom Clancy and Me"; and *Writing on the Edge*, "What the River Says."

"Teaching Tu Fu on the Night Shift" was reprinted in *The Questioning Reader* (Allyn & Bacon, 2000). "Letter to Ireland" and "Wiretap" (poem) were reprinted in *Forged Correspondences* (New Myths, 1996). "Wiretap" (prose version) first appeared in *To Prove My Blood: A Tale of Emigrations & the Afterlife* (Ashland Poetry Press, 2003). "The Elsewhere" first appeared in *Fathom* (Word Press, Cincinnati, 2007) and was reprinted in *The Elsewhere*, an online journal (www.elsewherejournal.org). "This Is Heyen

viii ACKNOWLEDGMENTS

Speaking" was chosen as a Notable Essay of the Year by *Best American Essays, 2008.*

Thanks also to the Ohioana Library Association for the Helen and Laura Krout Memorial Award; to the Ohio Arts Council for Individual Artist Fellowships in Criticism in 1999, 2001, and 2006; and to Youngstown State University for a sabbatical that gave me time to complete this book.

I am indebted to the writers' colonies which provided support and congenial work space during the writing of this book, including Fundacion Valparaiso, the Hambidge Center, Hawthornden Castle, the Headlands Center for the Arts, Ragdale, the Millay Colony, the Soros Center, the Tyrone Guthrie Centre, the Virginia Center for the Creative Arts, and Yaddo.

I offer deep gratitude for the inspiration and support of students and colleagues at the universities where I have taught, especially Armstrong College, University College Cork, the University of Delaware, Evergreen Valley College, the University of Ibadan, the University of Lubumbashi, Northeast Ohio MFA Program, San Francisco State University, Semester-at-Sea, SUNY Binghamton, Wilkes Low-Residency MFA, and Youngstown State University.

Special thanks to friends and colleagues who have read and commented on these essays: Chris Barzak, Robert Carioscia, William Heyen, Elsa Higby, H. L. Hix, William Greenway, Robert Lunday, Robert Mooney, Steve Oristaglio, Steve Reese, Jack Scovil, and Linda Strom.

And to my teachers, with affection and reverence—especially Robert Bly, Art Clements, William Dickey, Milton Kessler, Galway Kinnell, Richard Lanahan, Dan Langton, John Logan, Sean Lucy, John Montague, Stan Rice, Jerome Rothenberg, Michael Rubin, Barbara Shailor, W. D. Snodgrass, Ruth Stone, John Wheatcroft, and James Wright.

This book is dedicated to the memory of James F. Carens, friend and mentor. He began teaching me when I was eighteen, and never stopped.

Introduction

ON THE inside flap of his *Universitas Bucknellensis* algebra notebook, a freshman from Flushing, Queens, once wrote, "Mine is the soul of a bard."

Yes, I did. Sometimes, when a student comes into my office bearing aspirations, I recall that scrap of hubris and think, "Whatever's here can't be bad as that." And it never is.

But I'm deep into the process of forgiving my former self. After all, he was just expressing our cultural belief that poetry emerges from a kind of inspiration reserved for those special beings we dub "bards."

These essays come out of a life of teaching and writing which has revised my notion of poetry's source, of the places where it thrives and the purposes it may serve. As for bards—well, the seemingly audacious claim of this book's subtitle doesn't stem from birthright, but from an older definition of the name. Bards, in this ancient way of thinking, are a class of teaching poet, who simply pass on "the music of what happens," as they say. And that's what I've set out to do.

It's not that I no longer find poetry soulful, and I certainly don't think anyone can write well or read deeply without an immersion in craft. Poetry remains elusive: difficult to find, make, or teach. But I'm less likely to see inspiration rising out of my—or anyone's—selfhood. Like weeds cracking through asphalt, poetry wells up in the crevices, rupturing the slabs of the everyday to striate speech with song, tradition with resistance, and the visual with the ineffable. Evading definition by club, school, or institution, poetry is a kind of subversion that permits our vagrant selves to surface and blossom.

While they stem from particular occasions, these reflections cluster around three concerns. They begin in Youngstown, Ohio, a place that has given me plenty of opportunity to study sidewalk cracks. In 1990, I arrived as a new assistant professor in a town I'd never seen. All I knew was that my teacher, the revered poet James Wright, came from a burg just south of here. Since then, I've developed an allegiance to this region that Wright calls "Beautiful River"—in all its calamitous glory. "Heartland," proclaims the license plate, but I'm inclined toward "rust belt": a coarse, iridescent garment with a pungency missing from homogenous beltways. Maybe it's the weather (wetter than Seattle), or the hint of soot wafting from moribund steel mills. Maybe it's the grief that knits a town when thousands lose their jobs at once. With its iconic facades, stripped-down department stores, and traffic lights blinking over ghostly gridlock, Youngstown recalls Whitman's lines: "and if memorials to the dead should be distributed everywhere ... I should be satisfied." Youngstown's students too have taught me about the "in-between." Working full-time at low-paying jobs, living at home, caring for families, they bring to every classroom a sense of skepticism, worldliness, and humor. And what about the university itself, this jewel set in a toad's brow? Living here has made me question the place of the academy in a world where the vision of an ivory tower has crumbled.

The essays in the first section allude to other places which constitute my own personal rust belt, and the second section takes place in some of these locales. One such was Cork, a city named after a swamp. When I went there for my junior year abroad, Cork was something between a small city and a large village. Poets planted their elbows next to politicians; sheep grazed on the downtown soccer pitch; gossip sped faster than broadband cable. Over the years, I returned often enough that it almost seemed I had a second life in the city of swamp and gossip. And there was Lubumbashi, in the country known then as Zaire—where I taught as a Peace Corps volunteer at a university that had few books and spotty wiring. It is in places like these—far from the mainstream—that I've felt most at home.

Is there a reason why the oral tradition seems to flourish in back-waters? The essays in the second part of this book take up that question, celebrating a practice passed down from singer to listener, generation to generation. Whether set in a cottage in West Cork with the poet John Montague, or in low-life Ohio bars playing music with an Irish band, or in beehive huts on the West Kerry coast, these essays describe places where reciting a poem is as ordinary as passing on the news.

The essays in the last section, "The Poetry Broadcasting System," are preoccupied with another home—one not found on any map. Directing an independent literary press, running a university Poetry Center, designing a consortial MFA program, constructing my own books, and enjoying residencies at writers' colonies (including Yaddo—the setting of the last piece in this book), I've had some chance to weigh poetry's place in the world. When I hear that no one reads verse anymore, I think of the boxloads of submissions I've received as an editor; I think of the quiet, intense months spent with writers and artists from California to Prague; I think of the febrile gift economy of the small publishing world, which offers an alternative to the commodity-centered market. I think of all the poetry and music spoken and heard, entwining singer and listener, while giving both the opportunity to—in Tu Fu's words—"assent to their own spirits."

This book doesn't pretend to offer an overview of the landscape of pedagogy or poetics. Rather, it records moments in a solitary journey over broken ground toward an unknown destination. It's a book about the way we become most fully ourselves by passing things on: blending, amplifying, and refracting the past through the agency of a wayward genius that is deeply personal and as anonymous as breath.

Now that sounded good. I must have a bard's soul after all.

PART ONE

Teaching Tu Fu on the Night Shift

Teaching Tu Fu on the Night Shift

IT'S ONE of those prefab classrooms in the School of Business build-
ing that makes you feel like hooking on a straitjacket: pastel walls, pastel
desks, pastel carpet, no windows. Outside, the evening is warm—maybe
the last autumn evening before the rains and snow blacken this ghost steel
town for the next six months. But my students haven't seen much of the
day, or the evening, or even the fall for that matter: they've driven straight
in from suburban jobs, unwrapping a burger as they cruise for parking, or
plugging quarters into the basement snack machines before filing into the
elevator up to night class.

My father went to school like this—commuting from the 111th Precinct
in Queens to some ward room in Brooklyn where CUNY set up extension
classes for cops, putting himself through night school while he put me
through a country-club college as far away from Flushing as the moon.
What drove him, I was sure, was the need to see to it that the finger-
wagging over his TV tray in our squabbles about drugs, Napoleon, Viet-
nam, or Papal infallibility, still belonged to the upper hand.

Something must drive each student here to set aside two nights a
week for *English 638: Introduction to Modern World Literature:* a better job,
a child's respect, some undefined hunger. They're here to read, but more

importantly to succeed—or at least to keep a step ahead of failure—whatever it means and whatever it takes. And me? I'm far from home—here for the job and lucky to have it. So I tell myself.

But tonight, I saunter into English 638 feeling cocky—not just because I've strolled across this downtown campus on a balmy night savoring the year's last warmth, but also because I'm bringing to class the poems of Tu Fu, that wayward bureaucrat from the T'ang dynasty whose voice speaks directly to all of us in the Business building of a provincial university, where we obey "the summons to Court" that Tu Fu ignored, while "[his] colleagues paid respects to the Ministers of State." Yes, we're supposed to be studying Modern Literature, but tonight I'm feeling wayward, and I think this ancient Chinese poet assuages some longing our presence here attests to, a longing to understand how we have become cogs in a machine we can't smash. I think that Tu Fu, in Carolyn Kizer's elegant translations, confirms that others in distant times and places have faced the same dilemmas.

> Abandon me, all of you. This world does not suit;
> Not a court regular, unfitted for routine. . . .
> Well, well, I am demoted, and my dreams also.
> I may no longer look forward to Paradise.

In the poems that Kizer translates in *Carrying Over,* Tu Fu takes the measure of middle-class life and reveals the shame and anxiety afflicting workers and bureaucrats. The fact that Tu Fu's ninth century China is so familiar lends a whole new meaning to the word "modern."

> Swarms of flies arrive. I'm roped into my clothes.
> In another moment I'll scream down the office
> As the paper mountains rise higher on my desk.

But Tu Fu does more than scream out of office windows. These poems express angst, yet they are more remarkable for the balance they achieve between the quotidian world and the world of nature and spirit.

> Leaving the audience by the quiet corridors,
> Stately and beautiful, we pass through the Palace gates,

Turning in different directions: you go to the West
With the Ministers of State. I, otherwise.

On my side, the willow-twigs are fragile, greening.
You are struck by scarlet flowers over there.

Our separate ways! You write so well, so kindly,
To caution, in vain, a garrulous old man.

I love the tact of this poem, the way "stately and beautiful" is placed
ambiguously between Palace corridors and the pair of chastened courtiers.
I love the way the audience itself—Tu Fu's latest failure in sycophancy—
is passed over without comment in favor of compliments for the willow
twigs and scarlet flowers, and for the admirable writing of the vain cau-
tion. Finally, I love the way Kizer winks at Tu Fu's public persona, that of
"a garrulous old man," and reveals at the same time, by enclosing "in vain"
in commas, the dignity of his departure.

Harnessed to the working world, Tu Fu still revels in his own conflicted
nature: "Each day when Court is over, I skip to the pawnshop, / My nice
Spring wardrobe underneath my arm. / Bit by bit, I am drinking up my
clothes!" No romantic, Tu Fu weighs the dangers of bucking the system:
"I'll never see seventy now," he sighs; "Life is one, long, fragmented, murky
episode." While he gestures grandiloquently—"Sport with the women,
open the lavish hampers, / Guzzle the wine, gleaming and wet as rivers"—
he is as cagey as any salesman, winking from behind his ecstatic mask:
"High-sounding, isn't it? Come quickly then, / To my place, for now it just
so happens / I've saved enough small change to buy a gallon." I just know
my students will love this.

But after twenty minutes of coaxing discussion, after reciting some
choice poems, after spiraling into a peroration on suburbia, death, alien-
ation, pleasure, and just about everything short of Napoleon, I'm facing
raw silence. Not even Tommy Makem's tease to a tough audience, "Why
don't we all join hands and contact the living," gets a response. Well, it's
late; the students have been working for ten to twelve hours; their dinners
have come from machines, and their families are at home without them.
Still, I can't hide my disappointment.

Until tonight, we've been reading modern prose: Conrad and Lagerkvist, Anne Frank and Rosemary Mahoney. And up to now we've responded together—tracking Marlow through Conrad's jungly adjectives, leafing through Bullfinch to follow the allegory of *The Sibyl*, suffering with Frank, and sizing up Mahoney's China with a street-smart savvy. But tonight, I see the faces before me harden into masks I recognize: they look like me listening to my father—or not listening—just waiting for a pause so I could unleash the silence I whetted in my mind as he droned on.

Perhaps it's because Tu Fu is so relevant that they're uncomfortable; perhaps his irreverence stirs resentment in students still struggling to attain goals that Tu Fu scorns. He offers no "advancements," no "raises," no "hopes for the future." Indeed, it's tempting to consider him a drunken loser, and to place as much distance between his failure and our own hopes as a millennium and an ocean will allow.

But that's not it either. The class doesn't attack anything Tu Fu says: the discussion never gets that far. There's a lethargy tonight, edged with irritation. Though Tu Fu is as "gross and unrepentant" as ever, we hammer at his poems as if they were algebra problems.

"What does the willow stand for?" one student asks.

We trundle down the path laid out in high school and followed now by habit: Willow equals spring, spring equals renewal; therefore, willow equals renewal.

Finally, one student, wearing a tie and white shirt under his high school letter jacket, owns up.

"I don't like this kind of poetry," he says.

The class perks up.

"What kind do you mean?" I ask.

"Oh, I don't know—you know."

"Well, what do you like?"

"I like other stuff. Not old stuff. Stuff I can understand."

"You like contemporary poetry?"

Feeling picked on, he blurts out, "I like greeting cards."

Now everyone is alert. Some are amused, some almost offended; but the whole class seems intensely interested in what will happen next. It is as if a gauntlet has been thrown down. It is as if I stood up in front of the T.V. set and told my father his beliefs meant nothing to me. I realize that far from resenting a poet for thumbing his nose at the boss, my students seethe against authority as much as Tu Fu did. All the mindless memo-writing, all the orders followed, all the meaningless hack work: they detest it, and they retort with Tu Fu, "Could you learn to seed a furrow, and be free?"

But somehow, in this classroom, the tables have turned. Tu Fu doesn't speak for them; they and I are no longer critiquing a world together, as we were when we read Conrad and Mahoney. Now, for the first time, I am the representative of yet another authority: the authority of poetry—elitist, elusive, dangerous. While to me, reading Tu Fu seems liberating, to them it is another case of someone else holding the keys; and the gaudier my praise, the more they feel locked out. Now I see why this feels just like those quarrels with my father: the marshalling into position, the private silences. In praising Tu Fu, am I inviting the students to enter his world? Or am I just taunting them by offering a glimpse of a place they have worked to build but will not be permitted to enter?

Yet their yearning to break free is fierce. The greeting card the student received was called "Thanks." It was an acrostic, with interlocking rhymes, in a ballad meter.

> There's a rare and special quality
>   in the way some people live—
> However busy they may be,
>   they still have time to give.
> Anything you ask or need,
>   they'll do their very best,
> No matter what the task is
>   or how simple the request.
> Kindness just comes naturally
>   to this rare and selfless few,
> Special, giving people—
>   people just like you!

Listen to that: as rhetorically formal as its mauve calligraphy, and compared to Tu Fu, as certain as a commandment.

"What did you like about it?" I asked.

"It's personal," the student replied. "It came from a friend. It may not mean much to anyone else, but it's special to me."

What a beautiful way to read! The words' public meaning does not matter. On the Hallmark rack, this card is just another piece of merchandise. But when selected and mailed, the verses are infused with a private meaning; they are read in a completely new context in which my student's identity is acknowledged, even necessary. While the card may mean nothing to others, it gives the receiver an occasion to say, with Tu Fu, "I exult in selfhood, assent to my own spirit." As such, it challenges those who would try to shape personal taste without realizing that before poetry teaches or delights, we must first assent to self. We must first account for the fact of our own spirit.

This mercurial spirit is so strong that even Tu Fu, read in the context of university classes, is drained of the playfulness that makes his work so poignant. However simplistic the emotion of the greeting card, however much we know that it's created by people suffering the same disillusionment as we are—and soothing that disillusionment with a steady paycheck—read now it is plaintive, its very existence in the classroom a reproach to a system that records poems read, then doles out grades like promissory notes for a future with a happy face. Yes, there are days when, like my student and Tu Fu, I feel like saying, "Let them mark me absent." Studying in this pastel classroom with a group assigned here by computer saps Tu Fu of a quality that Yeats called "gaiety"—a joy that transfigures dread. Incredibly, Tu Fu becomes the cipher his poetry mocks.

At what point do we lose this gaiety? As children we know all about subversion. We mimic, we mock, we utter sounds fully confident of their personal meaning. What is the first poem most of us learn if not "NYAH, nyah nyah NYAH nyah?" And despite the fact that children's poetry has become an industry that churns out "age-appropriate" rhymes, children are not at all intimidated by the need to master meaning. They respond to poems regardless of reputation, and they often delight in poems adults fear. Recently, visiting a friend who reads poetry for pleasure, I listened as he and his seven-year-old daughter recited together:

> My fiftieth year had come and gone.
> I sat, a solitary man,
> In a crowded London shop,

An open book, an empty cup
On the marble table-top.

While on the shop and street I gazed
My body of a sudden blazed;
And twenty minutes more or less
It seemed, so great my happiness,
That I was blessed and could bless.

What could such a poem mean to a seven-year-old? Wrong question. Whatever thrill or comfort incanting its strange syllables affords, it will continue to change as her mind unfolds, and perhaps half a century from now it will recrystallize to yield yet another gladdening. Remembering my friend's daughter's sing-song recitation, I hear an echo of the poems, ballads, and jokes with which my father regaled me before we retreated into rival camps—everything from saccharine ditties to limericks I loved for their forbidden pleasure to Shelley's "Ozymandias." I absorbed them as naturally as another language whose meaning deepened as I grew. Even now I measure my growth by the light these and later poems shed; some of course have dimmed; others continue to brighten. Needless to say, my student's greeting-card doggerel won't change; "Thanks" won't continue to tickle his synapses once the pleasure of receiving it subsides; but maybe— just maybe—the satisfaction of revealing his personal longing in a poem he has claimed will give him a taste of the freedom poetic language offers. Maybe he will feel that poems he hasn't mastered might still belong to him as Yeats's "Vacillation" will always belong to my friend's daughter.

"A writer," says William Stafford, "is one who decides." So is a reader. At the point we allow others to decide for us what is good, we lose a vital sense of the transformative power of language. And when we apply to poetry the kind of discrimination that academia encourages, we jeopardize the very source of that transformation. I'm reminded of the "Peanuts" cartoon in which Charlie Brown wonders, "How do you know which poems to like," and Lucy replies, "Don't worry, somebody tells you." Greeting card, bad, we say. Tu Fu, good.

Perhaps not all of us lose the personal connection with the poetry we read. Perhaps those on top of the poetry food chain are able to maintain

that necessary sense that their feelings matter. Yet the ability to appreci-
ate a poem without relying upon some authority to tell us that the poem
is "good" is very rare. Most of us read with a censorious eye looking over
our shoulder, checking to see that we judge wisely. But as Robert Hass
observes, "Rhythm is at least partly a psychological matter." When we
change our minds, we change also the nature of the sounds we respond
to, and poems begin to move us not merely because they are mailed to
our address, but also because our sense of the personal is broadened to
include the dead and the living.

Poetry will be out of place in universities as long as it is treated as a
body of knowledge to be tested, as long as it is used to discriminate among
us rather than affirm some strand of being that we share, and as long as we
ignore what the great Irish hero Finn MacCumhal calls the finest poetry
in the world: "the music of what happens." It's a tune Tu Fu played—can
you hear it?—though he's too slippery for any syllabus.

Well, the next meeting was quite different. I was abashed; they were
contrite. We made it through the rest of *Carrying Over,* reading the poems
of Rachel Korn, Faiz Ahmed Faiz, Edouard Maunick, and Shu Ting—mod-
ern poets whose work was the reason I assigned this text. I left without
much idea if these poems touched anyone's life. But they touched mine.
After class, a student who enrolled because I had taught her daughter the
previous term showed me her favorite poem, called "I Am There." Written
by a man named James Dillard Freeman, it was carried to the moon by the
astronauts, and there it remains—a raft of paper floating in space.

Reading the poem—which she had found on e-mail—I think of Su Tung
Po, Tu Fu's poetic son, who looked into his wine cup, "full of the moon,
drowned in the river." I think how alone each of us is, how impossible it
is to reach across this vast impersonal space, and I realize now that my
father didn't finish night school to compete with me, but to feed a hunger
I could never fathom. He died earlier this fall, and seeing the faces of my
students struggling with Tu Fu, I feel a hunger I can never satisfy: to join
hands in the undertow of time and the unconscious—Tu Fu, my father,
myself, my students—though they are not my children, not at all.

Books of Sand

A Review of Unpublished Manuscripts, One a Conceit of Its Author

There are whole books praised and never read.

—RAEBURN MILLER

BORGES, says Frank, went one further. He praised books that were never written. Phantom books. Make-believe authors. And this is not off point, since Frank himself, letter of acceptance from Miami University Press in hand, threatens to decline their offer to publish his manuscript, thus joining the ranks of the make-believe, the phantom, the unpublished.

"It's unheard of," I say.

"Yes," says Frank, "I suppose I will be."

Frank Polite is not exactly my father, but if you're a poet in Youngstown— and what else can you be with unemployment what it is?—you're pretty much Frank's bastard. He has a real son, Khepri, by his first wife, who once played the sexy Zenite mining alien in a *Star Trek* episode. No, now that I think of it, Khepri belongs to Frank's second wife, the jazz singer. I met her at a local speakeasy; Frank introduced her as "the mother of my son." That's Frank. Only he can get away with tweaking ex-wives.

"They just want to mother me," he shrugs.

Frank saw Borges read once, and during the question period he felt the need to be recognized as a fellow human by this great man and so stood up and caught the attention of the sighted translator and asked Borges what he thought of Yeats.

"Stupid!" Frank spluttered, telling the story, to ask Borges, this Homeric presence, what he thought of another writer.

Then Frank's face lit up as if he himself were blind, delivering Borges's reply: "Thank you for linking my name with a name of such greatness."

Some days in this ex-steel town, it's hard to link our names to anything great. Hard to imagine Borges or Yeats or Captain James T. Kirk are members of our species—which, I suppose, makes *Hyde* a trope for Youngstown, as a place and also as a cankerous worry inside each of us, no matter where we live.

Hyde: A Novella Noir is Frank's book-length manuscript of pantheras, "an obscure poetic form / developed in Kang- / al-Sivas region of Turkey," as one panthera reveals. "A panthera lurks & leaps / jolting its prey into / a dazed clarity." This is a region Frank knows well—both the daze and the clarity—having once fled a job in the Human Resources Department of Mahoning County to live in Turkey. Turkey has become for Youngstown poets a kind of sister city (our imagination is expansive if fuzzy) from whence at least one pilgrim, George Peffer, has reported. George needed a vacation from "the hard work of living." His review: "We all choke on misapprehended hope."

Misapprehended pilgrimages are *Hyde*'s métier. Beginning in ancient Egypt; migrating to Las Vegas; on to Malabar, a hideaway in Ohio where Bogie and Bacall were wed; and finally ending in the "Holy City of Trebizond," *Hyde*'s protagonist "lurks & leaps" through language, an elusive principle of calm in a kaleidoscope of exotic trash. In this town we take our trash straight up. The other day I found a note stenciled on a cardboard sign in the window of a derelict building: "When you love a place, really and most hopelessly love it, I think you love it for its signs of disaster, just as you come to realize how you love the particular irregularities and even scars on some person's face." The words are attributed to "James Wright, Ohio poet."

Ohio poet indeed! James A. Wright was one of the greatest poets in English since Yeats. There's something beatific about the appearance of these lines so near their source. Having made the journey from Martins Ferry to Florence and international fame, they return, not as the lines from a famous poet, but as the words of a citizen haunting a place badly in need of naming. It's this kind of harebrained compassion for personal disaster that impels *Hyde* on its pinball-spin across centuries and continents, all the way to the oblivion of an unpublished manuscript.

The reason Frank decided to withdraw *Hyde* from Miami University Press is that they offered him "a contract from hell."

"How's that?" I asked.

"They take copyright, the movie rights, they even skim a percentage off any readings I give."

"Why didn't they offer you a standard contract?"

"Well, it is the standard contract, but *Hyde* isn't a standard book."

One thing's certain: Frank's not the standard author. There's something loopy about worrying about movie rights for a manuscript of poems, but as Frank points out, why not? "I'm sixty-two years old. I don't belong to any university. I don't care if I get brownie points from AWP. There's no real money involved. I'll just publish it myself if I have to."

Loopy, to me, louring in a provincial outpost of academia where news of publication seldom reaches. Yet sensible, too. It's an exercise of one of the few privileges that the ghetto economy of poetry allows. Frank offers a sane response to a state of affairs in which thousands of poets struggle to sell books no one reads.

Nor is this Frank's first brush with oblivion. There's the story of Miro Papadakis, the poet from the island of Skyros. Frank received a letter from this rural bard—through what agency, God knows—inviting him to meet the great man and to "adventure" with him and translate his works. After coaxing a local politico to muscle a grant from the Ohio Arts Council, Frank made his way to Greece. His halting Greek was no bother; it wasn't long before he found a bilingual collaborator with flowing dark hair and island eyes.

The "adventure" started beautifully. Papadakis was a fireplug in a caftan. Wildly hospitable, he caroused with Frank from noon till midnight, sloshing ouzo in his hut on the side of a rough mountain. Although he composed his poems orally (he had in fact never written them down at all), he employed complex stanza forms that seemed to recall the dactylic hexameter Homer had heard in the sea foam. His images, his intensity, and his simplicity were rooted deep in Greek soil; yet the demotic Greek was vivid as jazz. Few knew this iconoclastic bard, and fewer, Frank believed, appreciated his genius. Frank hoped to produce a volume of these translations.

Then one morning Papadakis disappeared. Frank climbed the mountain path to his hut to find the poet had vanished. No note, no good-bye. Lost at sea? Apotheosized? Fled a jealous husband? No one knew. Frank was left with a handful of scrawled poems, the dregs of his Ohio Council grant, and a nubile translator. "Four Translations from Miro Papadakis" were all Frank could save. They appear in his book, *Letters of Transit.*

Who can trust a fugitive, or a translator, or a poet in transit, or even their own judgment these days? Would I be writing this, or you reading it, if *Hyde*'s worth weren't confirmed by some poltergeist lurking in the basement of the English Department of the University of Miami? Even Lauren Bacall declined to read it. Frank wrote her, explaining that his forthcoming book of poems was set in Malabar, the Ohio resort where she'd married Bogie. Would the great lady accede to read the manuscript? Perhaps write a short blurb? A stamped card was enclosed for her convenience. On the card, Frank had typed "Yes/No," with two boxes to check. Frank read the letter aloud at the monthly open reading at the Cedars bar, a country western beatnik festival of bathos. He held the card up for all to see, the card touched by Lauren Bacall, the card with the penciled checkmark under 'No.'

"She could have at least written it out," says Frank. "You know how to say 'No,' don't you baby? Just put your lips together and blow."

Though I pose as a son, I have reached the age when manuscripts have more adventures than I do. In a place like this, the real rift isn't between Fathers and Sons or between Town and Gown; it's between Word and Flesh. Our manuscripts live the lives we've missed. Every poet has a tale. Like urban legends, they follow the same plot, having to do with close calls and dying editors. Our manuscripts flit around the world, seeking danger, avoiding certain death with the luck and cunning of James Bond. There's the writer who left Youngstown for Boston and lounged so long in Cambridge cafes that when his manuscript was accepted by Knopf he turned them down because word on the cobbled streets was that it's a

bad idea to debut with short stories. There's the poet who was so afraid
for his manuscript's safety that he would mail it ahead when he planned
a plane trip in case the plane went down. There's the poet who was prom-
ised publication right before the editor was indicted, and the poet whose
reputation was ruined because another poet of the same name circulated
dreck. The stories go back to Nora saving *Stephen Hero* from the fire and
beyond, harkening to the Old Testament mystery of the lost ark.

It's Flesh versus Word all the way down. Word claims that all you have
to do is live until you're thirty and then hand over the adventuring to the
manuscript. "As for living," says the French aesthete, Villiers-d'Isle, "our
servants will do that for us." Or in our case, our students. You can burrow
into the academy, get a PhD (with an oxymoronic "creative dissertation")
and live in the cloud-cuckoo land miles above the Zenite mines where
Frank's first wife panted her fifteen minutes. We too have our poets—
eighteen feet of us: William Greenway, Steve Reese, and me. PhDs and
manuscripts in hand, we landed in Youngtown from far parts—first
William, then Steve, and finally me, careful not to swamp the boat. William
placed two books with Breitenbush, and when they folded he managed the
next four with U. of Akron. Steve's manuscript was taken by Cleveland
State, and my second, after collecting more rejections than a smuggler's
passport, won a small prize from Ashland Poetry Press. Ah, the stories.
The strokes of luck. The almosts. The could-a-beens. Of course we submit
(perfect word) to all the unread journals, from *Poetry* to *Twenty Million
Flies Can't Be Wrong*, even though there's not a penny in it, and some days
we doubt if even the featured authors themselves read any but their own
poems. We're inveterate contest entrants; our entry fee tab tops our bar
bills. But we can afford it. Youngstown's cheap, and short of the mayor,
we've got the cushiest jobs in town.

Fed up with stamp-licking, Flesh ripostes that to be a poet you have to
leap out of the ivory tower chuteless. You have to travel to Turkey, work
years in the Human Resources Department of the third cornice of hell,
marry passionately and often, lose sleep and bleed pantheras. You have
to, in a word, suffer.

In the suffering, one's identity is purged. "The intellect of man is forced
to choose," says Yeats, "Perfection of the life, or of the work / And if it take
the second must refuse / A heavenly mansion, raging in the dark." But

Yeats also applied for the job of Professor at Trinity College just in case. He didn't get it.

Raging in the dark, few attain Yeats's stature. Most just get the suffering. But the belief that personal experience lends a necessary credibility to poems that we would not expect from fiction is an attractive idea, especially when the suffering looks compulsory anyway. Youngstown may be the official U.S. capital of poetic suffering.

There's a need here to shoot yourself in the foot, as if success might spoil your soul. *Hyde*'s gift for *duende* aside, Youngstown poets regularly maul whatever poor chances for the poor version of success poetry holds out. Sometimes it seems like a stampede toward invisibility, a collective yearning to rhyme the ghost smoke of dead steel mills. Or perhaps it's just a desire to return to a home whose name has been lost.

For instance, there's Ed Curley. A professional house-sitter, Ed describes a safe orbit around the university, enrolling in, but seldom finishing, courses in a basketload of subjects. Once at a reception for a visiting poet, he spent the better part of the evening in my bathroom, and after he finally stumbled out I found the sink plugged with Curley flume. This, I suppose, in application to house-sit. And why not? Come sabbatical or June, the faculty is so desperate for any sort of scarecrow to stand sentinel that Curley's services are always in demand.

As far as I knew, Curley's poetic career consisted of his monthly performances at the Cedars's open readings, where he operates as "Leo Rude." The pseudonym not only pays tribute to Frank but also describes the poems Curley reads—fragments from Catullus, Verlaine, and Bukowski, along with lintballs pulled from his own pockets. So I got quite a shock returning home after a stint of his house-sitting to find that Curley harbored poetic ambitions in his own name.

A few days after he'd moved on to his next target, my phone rang and a woman's voice—cultured, New England—asked for Mr. Curley. I explained that he no longer lived here and left no forwarding number.

"Well, if you do find him, could you ask him to call Maxine Kumin?" And she gave me a number that whirred and jumbled in my head.

"*The* Maxine Kumin?" I blurted out.

"How kind," replied the voice.

"If you don't mind my asking, Ms. Kumin, how do you know Ed Curley?"

"We've never met," the famous poet responded, "but he sent me a letter with a wonderful poem about Alexander Pope. He left this number. I was just calling to thank him. I hope I'm not disturbing."

Disturbing? My world was turned inside out. I conjured up the bulbous head of my house-sitter, his Camel slouch. Hard to imagine he'd written anything that wouldn't fit on a cocktail napkin. But curiosity gnawed, and I drove down to the Cedars and nabbed Curley—who probably thought I meant to pester him about a cracked dish—and I asked for and received a copy of the poem Maxine Kumin praised.

It's a poem of several hundred lines divided into two sections. The first section, composed of heroic couplets, pastiches the elegant vitriol of Pope. Addressed to the poet who "considered with a cast eye what dissolves, who assessed bitterness and scale," the poem echoes Pope's contempt for poetasters, quoting a line from "Epistle to Dr. Arbuthnot" about a versifier so addicted to rhyming that "lock'd from ink and paper, [he] scrawls / with desp'rate charcoal round his darken'd walls." The second section veers into another kind of prosody—long syllabic lines laced with internal assonance, describing a contemporary of Pope who died virtually unknown in a debtor's prison in Ireland. He went by the formidable name of Cathal Buidhe MacGiolla Ghuna, and if he's known at all today, it's for Thomas MacDonough's translation of his poem "An Bannan Bui" ["The Yellow Bittern"]. Curley balances these two worlds—one enlightened, one verging on oblivion—to suggest that the enlightenment fed on the neighboring darkness, that light in fact leeched its power from truths incubated in darkness. The horror of the poem stems from the revelation that Cathal Bui, according to legend, scrawled his last poems on his prison walls in charcoal.

Maybe ours is such: a necessary darkness. Maybe we in Youngstown are figures in a dusk without which the belief in a poetry which emerges from a select cadre into the light of publication would disintegrate. Perhaps our role is to remind that every literature course ought to assign at least one book that is not a book. Every bookstore ought to feature empty shelves.

And in case this essay in its published form reflects too much glare, I have taken the precaution of including two poets who do not exist. One was Frank's invention. There is no Miro Papadakis. In a modern day version of MacPherson's scam, Frank invented the Greek poet for the sake of the state grant. The great adventure was a yarn woven with Frank's customary flourishes deep into a Cedars's endless evening. The four Papadakis poems that appear in *Letters of Transit* were his own compositions, rendered afterward into Greek by his beautiful translator.

The poet Curley, with a bow to Borges, I have made up myself.

Tom Clancy and Me

MY BROTHER is one cool dude: six foot two with shoulders to thrill doorways, a Cheshire cat smile, and skin that must be rained-down satin. He's a salesman who clears well over a hundred grand, and if it weren't for a weak jump shot, he could have played big-time college basketball. Look up the word *Luck,* and you'll find his name: he married his college sweetheart and they live in a mansion in Bucks County; he has a beautiful daughter (my goddaughter) and a son who seems to have inherited his father's gifts for a charmed life.

And yet, though I am single with a past that only a chess master could outmaneuver, though I make a sliver of his salary, though I live in an apartment in a ghost town in the Midwest, somehow our lifelong competition hasn't sputtered out. I'm still the elder, and the sledgehammers I held over him in our childhood still have weight.

His catchphrase, when I describe my life as an academic, is, "You have too much time on your hands."

He both respects and dismisses the life. He accepts that my work as a poet will never sell (still, he's cooked up quite credible marketing schemes); but it irks him that I spend so much time writing poems (which, if they ever bobbed into the mainstream, would merely befuddle or bore), when

I could be putting my skills to more practical uses—like writing thrillers, or mysteries, or even greeting cards.

Reading my poems, my brother is silent, since many of them are about our lives together. But he's upset when I lie. "Is this supposed to be Uncle Ed? He didn't shoot himself; you can't write that." And what can I say? Never will I have so intense a reader. How can I tell my brother that I change facts to make truth? How can I tell him that I don't care how many readers I have, only how deep?

I often drive to see him and his family. It's seven hours on the turnpike, which seems like an eternity of bumpers and McDonalds. Lately, I've taken to listening to books on tape bought at truck stops. It helps. For the next seven hours, I'm enthralled in some mystery, the lifeline so appealing that sometimes I actually drive around some more before I get to my brother's house. While the world of pop fiction seems completely removed from mine, it provides one of the few occasions we iconoclasts have to appear good-natured and democratic: "Hey, did you read Dennis Rodman's book?" "Oh yeah, it was great."

Over the Brady family recipe for quarrels—prime rib and Rusty Nails—I once dropped the prole bit and began squeezing a Tom Clancy novel in ways it wasn't meant to be squoze: Style, language, etc.

My brother sneered: "Yeah, well, Tom Clancy could have your job in a New York minute."

That put a stop to my gallop. He's right, of course. But I'm in no danger of losing a gig at a state school in the Midwest to a multimillionaire who once tried to buy the Minnesota Vikings.

But the thought still galls. Is it true Tom Clancy could do my job—even if he'd want it? Is it true that market forces hold sway in academia? Would the quality of higher education be enhanced if we quadrupled faculty salaries, thereby enticing phenoms to make a killing? Are we enmeshed in the same web as other professionals—and a lot closer to the spider, considering our pay? In other words, are the people who work in business, medicine, and law better than academicians in the same way our culture believes they're better than anyone else who makes a slice of their salary?

Of course, it's difficult to compare academic training and selection to comparable practices in other sectors of the economy. Education in the liberal arts traditionally has been a magnet for the feckless. Hence the belief that "non-professional" graduate school is "soft." My mother, a school secre-tary in Brooklyn, used to call the PhD "piled high and deep"; she also claimed she could tell a school psychologist just by his shuffling gait. Law school, medical school, business administration—these are the "hard" degrees, and those who grind those mills deserve, the thinking goes, more money.

Yet while I haven't been to law school or med school, I'm not sure that the training they offer is more challenging than liberal arts graduate edu-cation, though it may be more grueling. It's true that these professional schools tend to cull candidates more rigorously than liberal arts graduate schools do, and it is probably also true that they grade more strictly. I'm reminded of one English professor who told me he never failed anyone. "Let life fail 'em," he used to say. But to compare grading curves is to fall into the trap of judging one kind of education by the standards of another. In the liberal arts, real achievement is rare. It can't be graded; sometimes it can't even be recognized. Embarking on this voyage means taking enor-mous risks, inviting—even expecting—failure. After all, what kind of fools would put themselves through five to ten years of graduate work knowing that at the end there's only a small chance of getting a job in their field? And real success takes a lifetime, not a term. As Dante says, entering Para-dise: be sure you have a sturdy boat if you want to follow any further.

Yes, Tom Clancy could have my job. The students would be pleased. For one thing, they've heard of him; and for another, they wouldn't even need to listen to the books—they could see the movies. And what, besides the fact that he would never take a job teaching at my salary, would keep Tom Clancy from being the best candidate?

What is it exactly that we offer—we, the tenured, the unread, who don't (as much as we may want to) work at market value? Well, the Rusty Nails weren't conducive to forming an articulate response, but since then I've thought soberly about that conversation with my brother.

What I've come up with is this: Academia offers another way of judging value, counter to the market system.

The Sumerians invented two number systems, I'm told: the decimal system, which they used to count how much grain was stored and how many soldiers were on call, and a system based on numbers that cor-responded to human faculties and infinity—numbers that didn't *count*, but had a value nonetheless. In academia, our value system is based not on money, but on time. We're paid less than others who've gone through fewer years of schooling are paid. But though our pay is low, when I talk to my friends in the business world about my schedule of three classes each semester, about my term off for a Research Professorship, about my upcoming sabbatical, they are both envious and appalled. Ignoring the discrepancies in our salaries (one friend figured he makes my yearly gross in three days), they feel I'm somehow cheating the system.

Even our own administrators seem to feel this way. The other day a dean rolled his eyes at me, complaining about how much time we professors get off. I half agree. I do think it's better to make my own schedule than to have a hefty salary. I've watched my friends struggle in New York's business world; I've seen the compromises, the burden of being at someone else's service, of being a "Human Resource." And when I take stock, I say willingly, "Show *them* the money."

Perhaps my friends are right to suggest that in exchange for higher pay we ought to teach eight hours a day. Perhaps the iconoclastic journals, the unattended presentations, and the unpronounceable colloquia are boondoggles. Maybe we can "cut the fat" and even get raises. What's disturbing to me is not that such an argument has merit, but that it would gain so much credit within our own profession. I hear a lot about being underpaid, but very little about the fact that we have been granted what no other secular group in American society has: equal amounts of freedom and responsibility.

What's disturbing is what we do with it. I have nothing against the arcane essays; I applaud them. When someone says that no one cares about such things as Medieval quilting or anagrams from Villon to Dr. Seuss, I think of Yeats excoriating the Abbey Theatre mob who screamed down O'Casey's *The Plough and the Stars:* "You have disgraced yourselves again." I think of Maxine Kumin saying that she always writes for that "perfect audience of one." I think of Blake seeing "an immense world of delight" in "every bird that cuts the airy way." I think of a thousand moments when my internal landscape has been transformed by "arcane" research.

But sometimes in a committee meeting I see more of the crowd Yeats cowed than of the players who ducked vegetables behind him. Sometimes English Department meetings sound a whole lot like business meetings, with a whole lot less at stake; we gabble about requirements, grade distribution, meeting community needs. If we are going to run our universities this way, maybe we ought to demand bureaucrats' salaries.

I'm not suggesting that we not "meet the needs" of the community, or that we not run our shop efficiently; I'm not suggesting that we abandon attempts to redefine ourselves as our culture redefines itself. Our occupation is entwined with all others. I'm suggesting that we bring to bear on these redefinitions the unique perspectives we are blessed with. Let's not place salaries above independence; let's remember we're a faculty, not just a bargaining unit.

Our paltry pay is a lynchpin, keeping our lives different from the lives of doctors, lawyers, businessmen. What drives graduate students to immerse themselves in little-known fields of study is not an expectation of reward (though they may hope for it); rather, the driving force is passion. I remember Galway Kinnell saying that Whitman and Melville shared two typical characteristics of American writers: stubbornness and stupidity, lighted with genius. I remember W. D. Snodgrass saying that when students ask if they should devote their lives to poetry, he replies, before looking at their poems, "Not if you can be happy doing anything else." I believe that the system that rewards graduates of professional schools with high salaries and makes itinerant workers of many PhDs in the liberal arts may be unfair, but changing it to fit a professional paradigm might very well sap the liberal arts of some essential vitality, and so deprive our culture of an entire means of perception.

Faculty. Think about the word: an ability, a way of perceiving. Our responsibility is not merely to produce graduates, but to follow our quirky obsessions, to live untrammeled intellectual lives which validate our time, if not our salaries. David Quammen says he refuses to watch the Super Bowl because one day our culture may need someone who's never witnessed it. It may seem unlikely, but it may be that our culture needs a secular institution which embodies a value system where passion, fancy, and even failure, if aspirations have soared, have an honored place.

Teaching Like My Fathers

I GREW up thinking that my father was smarter than my mother, and recently, while talking to my mother on the phone, I found out that she spent most of their fifty-two years of marriage thinking the same thing.

"Why?" I asked. "After all, I was just a kid, so it was natural for me to think that he was the intellectual, going on at the dinner table about Esperanto and Aquinas while you dished out the casserole. Why did you think he was so smart?"

"Because he told me he was," replied my mother.

I can just see it. He didn't tell her straight off. There would have been no insult; it would have come after some declamation or quip, and the condescension would have fallen softly as mist. After all, whatever gifts he had were hers too. Probably she wanted him to claim the brains because it made her feel safe.

What's ominous to me is that today my fiancée gazed into my eyes and told me how smart I was. How good this felt until it hit me that with all the poems I'd spouted, she must have thought that's exactly what I needed to hear. It's not just her. Yesterday I found a cartoon taped to my office door by an anonymous wag. It shows a man gesturing behind a podium, a butt hanging from his lip. In the foreground, a woman gripes: "He specifically said dinner and dancing—there was no mention of his poetry."

By what Oedipal paths have I become the father I intended to flee? He was a New York cop, so I became a poet. He backed Wallace, so I became an anarchist. He barbequed London broils, so I became a vegetarian. He hated blacks, so I went to live in Africa. Only lately have I realized that there wasn't any real rebellion in all this. It didn't matter *what* I did; what mattered was *how*. Our entwined fates can be spooled out in almost any setting.

The teachers I admired most seemed like amplified versions of my father. I remember James Wright, in the last year of his life, leaving the classroom every half-hour to cough in the hallway, only to return, pocket his handkerchief, and launch into a Yeats poem or a vaudeville skit. I drank in every word. Only once that semester did he address me personally (until then, I hadn't thought he knew my name), and that was after having asked us to write "beautifully" in an in-class essay.

"Why are you smiling, Mr. Brady?" he asked.

Replaying that scene now, I respond with Beardsley: "Because beauty is so difficult." But at the time, of course, I merely blushed and shrugged.

I remember W. D. Snodgrass looking like Isaiah and sounding like "Henry Pussycat" as he ran the scales of his tenor voice through Berryman's *Dream Songs*. Sometimes he'd stop mid-poem to say things like, "Donald Hall is the first poet to learn from Whitman," or "It's easy to see now that Delmore Schwartz was not a poet." He'd make these pronouncements suddenly, as if they'd just occurred to him, then dive right back into a poem. To me it seemed he was breathing some other air. I remember John Logan breaking the awed silence that followed his recitation to confess: "My students keep me alive." Needless to say, we felt inadequate to the task. But I wonder now if he didn't mean that it was the ghosts of his own teachers that kept him, for a while, alive. I know how he felt.

These teachers seemed visitors from some planet where wisdom had been earned on "the crooked roads" that Blake calls "roads of genius." Still, however distant their origin, their presence was not foreign; I was feebler, and perhaps I would never achieve their greatness, but shamelessly I felt akin to these great men.

So the readings I give are all from memory (one friend says I sound like a missionary bishop), and when I teach I'm never more than an awkward silence away from erupting into a poem or dusting off an old joke. I seldom prepare for class beyond taking a long walk; I never know exactly what will happen. But after thirty years of teaching, I know *something* will happen. For me, it's a spontaneous group improvisation, and I see myself passing on what was passed on to me by teachers whose extemporaneous brilliance filled me with longing to be like them.

Yet how do others see me? One problem with sounding like a missionary bishop is that people pay more attention to the voice than to the poem. The first comment from people who hear me recite is almost always the same: "How do you remember all that?" I assure myself that these comments annoy me, that I want people to remember the poems, not the poet. But lately, thinking of my father, I realize that I invite this praise.

Of course when I say *people* I mean *women*. What was it my father and I sparred over every evening at the dinner table if not the approval of my mother? How we appealed to her, each of us taking any reservation she expressed as a trumpet call to further eloquence.

I was babbling on about all this over lunch with a female colleague who half-admired, half-resented the ease with which I seemed to teach. Like me, she had studied in traditional programs, listening to tweedy men soliloquize. Yet she felt she could never be like them. Their brilliance only reinforced her sense of inadequacy. Just as I have been driven by my teachers' examples, she was driven to overcome the self-doubt they had unintentionally instilled in her.

She prepares extensively for every class, writes comments on student papers that must take longer to compose than the papers did. Yet she feels ill at ease making judgments. Moreover, my colleague tells me that she feels students *expect* a different approach from her than from me. While they may forgive my devotion to what Michael Longley calls "the higher nonsense," from her they expect outlines, detail, and linear thinking. They expect, in the parlance of deans and politicians, "accountability."

Accountability to what, I wonder? Perhaps to a tradition of which my colleague was never invited to partake?

One irony here is that at first glance our experiences seem to run counter to our cultural stereotypes. Isn't it women who are supposed to access the anonymous, the subconscious, the lyric? Men are supposed to be separate, autonomous, linear.

But our experiences reflect the allure of these stereotypes. Yes, the muse is feminine, but the male channels inspiration, gives it *logos* and the technology of language. Inspiration can only take place if a structure is assumed—and the structure is masculine.

What's more insidious is that while the turbine of the male-dominated power structure hums strongly in the worlds of business and politics, in the university its workings are often muffled. My friends who majored in business have for the most part slipped easily into their fathers' well-heeled shoes, but my male colleagues don't look so empowered. We don't gavel meetings; we teach non-sexist language; we take afternoon naps. Our department chair, both our composition coordinators, and our dean are all women. So it would be easy to think that we are transforming the power structure. We explode the canon; we feature women's studies; we trumpet multiculturalism. Of course, the texts we teach matter, and change is only possible if students can see reflections of themselves in the works they read. But what matters as much as *what's* taught is *how* it's taught; and as long as women feel pressure to meet bewildering expectations, the stereotypes of the powerful male and nurturing female will remain locked in place, no matter what texts are taught.

And it's not just women, but anyone who experiences the patriarchal figure as "Other" who is likely to feel silenced.

Teaching English literature at the University of Lubumbashi, I recited Whitman, Williams, and Ginsberg to a class of Zairian students. While African students were more prepared than Americans for this kind of spectacle, I wondered what they gleaned from listening to this *msungu* exude ardor for a literature celebrating democracy? What was I to them but a tourist from a place they studied but could never see? How was I passing on what my teachers had given me?

"It's more important to read than to write," Galway Kinnell told us, and Jerome Rothenberg said, "I write those poems that I have not found elsewhere and for whose existence I feel a deep need." Like my teachers, I believe that when we read literature we immerse ourselves in that great river of which all partake, and which partakes of us. Yet it is perhaps because I am a man, and a white man at that, that I am free to dip into that river and feel that by doing so I "contain multitudes."

It turns out that things are skewed in such a way that what binds us closest to others also keeps us trapped in our separate skins.

I'm not ready to abandon my teachers, some of whom are now members of what Homer and Spiro Agnew called "the silent majority" (Homer meant the dead; God knows what Agnew meant). I still believe something can be passed on. Yet I'm more likely now to wonder how the people (read women) in my classes relate to me from their vastly different points of view. In the process of imparting my enthusiasm, I don't want my students to focus on *me*, but on the works that speak through all of us.

Yet even the fact that I feel free to change and adapt reminds me of our differences. My female colleague feels no such freedom; even if she changed her spots to become one of the "creative types, with their heads in the clouds," as our secretary dubbed me when I botched some doleful administrative procedure, her students would resist. In her, absentmindedness would be called neglect; digressions condemned as irrelevancies. Would the silence that greeted her pronouncements be awed or sullen?

I don't have an answer, but I'm not satisfied with the answers I've heard. Curriculum reform is underway, but even the phrase *curriculum reform* has a soporific sound. I don't believe these problems can be addressed primarily by committees or departments—partly because it's the committee-and-department mentality that chains us. One thing I learned from my teachers is that I have the freedom to ignore committees and departments, that "like a laughing string / Whereon mad fingers play" I can "be secret, and exult," because in me my fathers exult too.

"All revolutions ought to be as slow as chemical changes in the sun," Yeats says elsewhere; but I feel a need for a smaller, more personal violence, an awakening of respect for the mothers who nurture us, without whom all eloquence is mere show. Let us celebrate the many kinds of teaching that shape us, and let those styles interpenetrate. I feel the need for a revolution that might take place during a walk from office to class on a spring day. Maybe that day, a line of Muriel Rukeyser will pass through a teacher's mind: "We are richly variable." And then she or I will open the class with Adrienne Rich's charge to all of us: "The worst thing of all / [is] not the crimes of others, not even our own death / but the failure to want our freedom passionately enough . . ."

What the River Says

MY COLLEAGUE Bill Mullen and I share birthdays, and every year we celebrate together. This past birthday was the best so far. In the shank of the evening, he slapped my present on the bar: a copy of his father's new book, a detective novel called *Behind the Shield.* I was delighted. I flipped through the pages under raffish lights, and spent the next two days immersed in that self-contained world novels open for us.

Behind the Shield is a sequel to Jack Mullen's first book, *In the Line of Duty;* both novels feature Sergeant Vincent Dowling, a crusty gumshoe struggling to maintain old-school standards in postmodern San Diego. While Dowling takes his place in the tradition of American hard-boiled sleuths, what distinguishes both of these novels is the craft with which Mullen delineates Dowling's personal drama. Working within the genre of detective "procedural" fiction, Mullen delves into his protagonist's psyche to make the formula register deeper concerns. Yes, Vincent Dowling always gets his man, but his character is complex; he is neither a Joe Friday stuffed shirt nor a Dirty Harry wannabe. Dowling's conflict stems from a personal tragedy—the suicide of his wife. Ironically, it is the detective's devotion to duty which endangers his family and, ultimately, his soul. Dowling's fate is Oedipus'; he believes he serves the people when in fact he is a patsy to his own hubris. That he cannot bring his wife back from the dead lends terror to his story; that he continues to struggle gives it human pity.

Perhaps Jack Mullen is able to work this material so movingly because writing has been a kind of redemption for him: like his alter ego, Mullen worked as a homicide detective in San Diego for twenty years, and only in midlife did he start his career as a writer. Jack began, as I think most writers do, by yearning. He began with the belief that his life made for a story well worth the telling. During his years on the Force, he kept notes on all his strange encounters, stuffing scraps of paper into his pockets and then emptying them each night into a bureau drawer. I don't know if Jack always intended to compile these notes into a novel, but clearly he felt a profound connection between life and storytelling.

What makes Jack different from most aspiring writers is his acceptance of the labor it took to make his experience compelling to others. When Jack submitted the first drafts of *In the Line of Duty* (titled *Be Ashamed to Die*—Avon insisted on the new title for commercial reasons), it was a far cry from the finished novel. But Jack kept at it, attending workshops and honing his craft after his retirement while moonlighting as a security guard. It took Jack Mullen ten years to finish his first book.

These two books mean almost as much to me as they do to my friend Bill. For one thing, Bill and I came to the Midwest from opposite coasts but similar backgrounds: we're both jocks; both Irish-Americans ("narrow-backs," my mother calls us—suggesting spinal weakness, as if the ocean voyage strained out all strong genes). But the biggest reason I feel personally involved in Jack Mullen's success is that my father was a cop.

Like Jack, my father always wanted to write a novel. He was a New York City homicide detective, twenty years on the Force, and he certainly had enough stories to write a corker. Over dinners, he'd regale us: the time a hit man put his piece to his target's head and pulled the trigger and the gun jammed and the killer laughed it off, "Vito, HA, that's something, me killing you." The hit man stopped the limo, stepped out, cleaned the gun, then got back in and finished the job. And there was the Alice Crimmins case—a Queens woman accused of murdering her two children. My father worked the case, and I have vivid memories of Alice Crimmins, murderess, sloshing cocktails in our living room while I peeked down from between the banister rails upstairs.

All it took, my father thought, to make a novel was to write it down. He even built a plywood desk and spent evenings in the basement. We heard him down there, clacking away on his Royal typewriter. But for all his experience and desire, he never wrote a novel.

So many composition students feel this same hunger. They see their lives in terms of story, believing they lack only the verbal skills to get it down. In their minds, thought and language flow entwined, but on the blank page the river freezes.

This feeling is especially frustrating for returning students, who bring a lifetime to the classroom. Many students have approached me wanting to write a book they have been carrying around in their heads. They are sure that all it would take is to get it down on paper. One student came into my office with the story of her divorce. Her husband had cheated on her for years; there had been phone-tapping and shady lawyers and hurled china. She recognized in her life the awful outlines of stories she had read; now all that remained was to plug her details into the conventional template.

A student in her seventies was even more enthusiastic about her project. She had never written poetry, in fact she had been "quite steady," but one day she was overcome by some sourceless grief. She found herself wondering if life were worth living. That evening she heard a radio show about Sylvia Plath, and she went to the library to read about this death-obsessed poet. Soon Plath was appearing to her in her kitchen—she recognized the specter from the book jacket photo. She must write this story, starting now.

Most composition teachers will recognize these students: we've all received essays which attempt to express unspeakable frustration. An eighteen-year-old freshman tells about being raped on a prom date; a man recovering from surgery begins an essay with a line worthy of Baudelaire: "My heart leaks blood." But of course these students discover, as my father did, that it's not merely a question of getting things down, even when your life story seems to follow a genre pattern.

Whether people who suffer trauma are more likely than others to devote themselves to writing I don't know. The yearning to write seems to haunt even people who've found other creative outlets. Irving Berlin writes, "The story behind 'This is the Army' is as good as the show itself. That story should be written, and I wish I could do it. . . . But writing a book is quite different—the mere thought scares me, and for a very good reason: it's not my racket. I haven't the tools, to say nothing of the talent. But I have the material for such a book." Berlin's diffidence reveals his insight into the nature of craft, gained from a career of making songs. His sense of the challenge facing all artists has been enlarged by immersion in his chosen field.

The question teachers face is whether or not to create in the composition classroom an atmosphere where students are encouraged to regard their lives as material for writing. Is it desirable, in a brief term, to embark on a journey writers take years to accomplish?

When Jack's first novel was finally in print, I invited him to give a reading at Youngstown State. I wanted to celebrate his remarkable success, and I thought my students would appreciate his labor and learn from his presence. So along with sponsoring a reading, I assigned *In the Line of Duty* in my composition class, and I asked Jack to visit the class.

The reading and the visit were wonderful. Jack enthralled the class, talking about his process, about the difficulty of facing the blank page, about revision and critiques, about peer groups and outlining. He confirmed for the students that writing was an activity, like any other. Pacing the classroom as if it were a squad room, Jack gave it to them straight, and I heard in his no-nonsense advice an echo of Yeats: "A line will take us hours maybe / But if it does not seem a moment's thought / Our stitching and unstitching have been nought." For that day, anyway, I felt a connection among writers of diverse genres: cop novels, Romantic poetry, expository essays. I felt that the source of these genres might be traced to the same hunger.

But while the students took to Jack and his book immediately, my colleagues were more wary. When the composition committee met to consider the idea of using texts by visiting writers in comp classes, the atmosphere was quite different from the one Jack had created in the classroom. One colleague questioned the idea of "privileging narrative" in a class meant to teach expository writing. She wondered how my students would fare in the research writing course that follows freshman composition. For her, writing detective novels was a completely different activity from writing expository prose, and while a novel might work in a creative writing class, it was, she felt, an inappropriate choice for composition.

Another colleague raised a different objection. He argued that it's wrong to use fictive models or to bring writers into class to talk about their writing habits and styles because the writing process is essentially mysterious; it can't be taught, and any attempt to prescribe it imposes the writer's idiosyncratic habits on students who must develop their own. The job of the composition instructor, he felt, is to allow students to develop a sense of style while also familiarizing them with the accepted structures and modes of exposition.

I listened; we thrashed it out. But later, thinking of how this ex-cop connected with a class of beginning writers, and remembering the lassitude I've encountered in other composition classes I taught in more traditional ways, I couldn't help but think that in teaching writing, I had to tap that source so many students had talked about. I had to help them give their mute experience a voice.

Perhaps this debate really comes down to what instructors want when we ask students to write. Teaching given forms, especially as they are given from the position of authority the teacher occupies, can reify these forms in students' minds. In our efforts to prepare students for success in the culture of the university and the marketplace, we might pave over the source that pulses beneath any kind of art: the desire to bring to the surface some portion of mind's terrain.

The difficulties here of course cut to the very essence of writing: illuminating the mind with form; invigorating form with sinewed thought. I'm reminded of John Donne's famous couplet: "I am a little world made cunningly / Of elements and an angelic sprite." Donne may have had in mind the division between body and soul, but there's also an echo of the cleft between the outer world of form and the nascent internal world of the "angelic sprite." When we introduce to students this creative conflict, we offer them the opportunity to striate their "angelic sprite" with their own personal elements. That seems a formidable objective for a composition course, and it's understandable that my colleagues are loath to undertake it, opting instead to teach what can be measured.

But I would argue that unless we connect the world of "elements" to the "angelic sprite," we can't teach the mechanics of essay writing any more than Miss Jeanne Brodie can teach Italian culture. Rather than learning mechanics, students learn instead that there is no interface between thought and craft. They learn that genres are sealed off from each other and from the students' native powers. They learn that writing expository essays is unconnected to writing novels, or poems, or letters, or newspaper columns. They learn that an ineffable thing called talent—which can't be taught—is the price of admission to any experience of joy in writing; and they learn that while we grant to those we classify as "creative writers" the freedom to try out their talent, we will not value or cultivate the voices of beginning composition writers, however potent their experiences may be.

Learning begins when some yearning is stirred. We can't ignore students' need to weave life into story, and we can't impose structures on them—no matter how many courses they take. I went through a bachelors, two masters and a PhD without shaking the stiffness off my prose style; writing term papers did little to help me develop a personal voice. Rather, I became, as many students do, a chameleon, blending into different classes by mimicking accepted forms. The only writing that I valued and published was poetry: a transgression, written at night. By making poetry, I slowly discovered the ebb and flow of form. It was only after I stopped being a student—at least in my own mind—that I began to feel that the prose forms I'd learned in school might also be crafted from within.

I think I could teach someone committed to saying something how to use a few given forms in a semester, but all the exercises in the world will only serve to alienate a writer whose passion isn't engaged. Teaching skills in the lockup that composition classes sometimes resemble makes students see us as bad cops.

Writing is not the natural expression of a life lived. No one, veteran or novice, transfers meaning directly from nervous system to page. Nor is craft imposed from outside; it is not a set of skills or rules; it is not a menu—comparison/contrast, cause and effect, detective novel, sonnet. If the genre students choose to write in doesn't allow them to channel the flow of language, then assignments merely confirm their sense that the system is wrong, or worse, that they are wrong, that their impulses have nothing to do with writing. Instead, if we take account of the students' stories, then genres fructify, and we hear an echo of *Oedipus the King* in *Behind the Shield*.

Teaching craft means nurturing that connection between the word and the life. Reading and writing stories can offer a place where students learn, as Jack Mullen did, that their lives can and must be remade in the re-vision that writing insists on.

I choose narrative instead of exposition as the access point because stories are the first experience students have with crafted language. Intuitive yet highly formalized, stories move all around us, yet they remain the mode of our most personal revelations. Writing stories allows students to make nonlinear associations and daring connections, to play.

Thinking about the challenge of teaching the source of genres rather than imposing forms, I recall William Stafford's poem, "Ask Me":

> Some time when the river is ice ask me
> mistakes I have made. Ask me whether
> what I have done is my life.

Stafford touches on the paradox that we are always living two lives—the one of events, and the secret one that makes us believe that however the events in our lives freeze into shapes, inside us our lives and stories coalesce. "We know / the current is there, hidden;" Stafford writes, "and there / are comings and goings from miles away / that hold the stillness exactly before us. / What the river says, that is what I say."

This is our task: to stand above the river of language and trust that the current is there, beneath the frozen surface of form. In doing this, we break through the constrictions of an imposed authority. We give students the chance to follow the many lines of narrative and causation that flow beneath the surface. We transgress creatively against any form that's imposed from the outside rather than heard and confirmed within.

In such a way, new writers can break out from many constraints: the five-paragraph essay that so many hold to their chests like a shield, the comparison essay, the exercise in freewriting, the journal. Yes, use them; but don't allow them to constrict that shadow self: the maker.

That such a journey takes far more time than a semester is obvious; no one would see the composition class as a novel-writing workshop. Perhaps, though, even an academic term is enough time to provide a glimpse of the larger landscape that delving into one's deepest concerns reveals.

We don't have ten years, and few students or instructors have the single-minded devotion to writing of a Jack Mullen. But the fact that our time is brief makes the task more urgent: most often, composition classes are the first and last exposure adults students have to writing. Can we afford not to introduce writing as a craft? Can we spend our time judging them by standards that writers themselves scorn? Perhaps students will decide to become songwriters, or mechanics, or accountants. But they will bring to those occupations a feeling of having touched an immensity. And perhaps their sense of craft in their chosen fields will be deepened by their experience of the connection binding all creative activity.

"The devil takes his time with those he's sure of," says Samantha Mulcahy, Dowling's Irish partner in *Behind the Shield*. And while the devil or muse has grabbed Jack Mullen by the nape of the neck, others are merely tapped, released, and saved for later—or for later generations. Though my father abandoned his novel, his desire was so powerful that it outlived him and was infused in me. And now I find myself standing above the river, feeling it flow beneath, and here within.

Entangled Music

RECENTLY in a course on contemporary Irish fiction, I paired Edna O'Brien's selected stories, *A Fanatic Heart*, with a film, Gillies MacKinnon's *The Playboys*, which is set in the same rural Ireland where many of O'Brien's stories take place. O'Brien's tortured accounts of love strip the heart of fantasies; the last lines seem to rise up from a deep stone well. "Christmas Roses" ends with an older woman fleeing her young suitor before a love affair could even start. The narrator of "The Love Object," who was not so circumspect, finishes her account of a failed love affair with: "I suppose you wonder why I torment myself like this with details of his presence, but I need it, I cannot let go of him now, because if I did, all our happiness and my subsequent pain—I cannot vouch for his—will all have been nothing, and nothing is a dreadful thing to hold on to." The most despondent lines of all close "Over," a ghastly suicide letter to a departed lover: "Write to me, let me know if you are married. I need to know; I will never know; I do not want to know now."

Sharing with O'Brien a concern for women betrayed by a parochial society, *The Playboys* follows a very different plotline. When "Tara" bears a child out of wedlock by the local policeman, she is harassed by the villagers and "read from the altar" by the parish priest. But she's saved when a group of traveling players cruises into town, and the most eligible rascal, played by

Aidan Quinn, falls in love with her, sweeping her off on his Harley to Dublin
—bairn and all.

Asking my students which vision they preferred, I was surprised to
hear that they found the film more believable. O'Brien's characters were
described as "helpless," "self-pitying," "crushed by life;" while Tara was
"self-actualized," "courageous," "exemplary." In short, the film was "uplift-
ing," while the stories were "depressing."

From one point of view, the stories *are* depressing: they offer no escape
routes and no chopper-knights. Perhaps my students had nothing in com-
mon with people trapped by illusions. Yet the class ranged in age from
eighteen to fifty; all, I suppose, had experienced some tragedy. As for love,
Youngstown's patterns of romance bear an eerie resemblance to those
detailed by O'Brien. Was it possible that none of these students recog-
nized themselves in O'Brien's heart-scalded characters? Perhaps that's
just it—they *did* recognize themselves, yet they rejected the grim images.
And in any case, the chords struck by O'Brien's prose seemed so universal
that any adult could hear them.

But the students talked hardly at all about O'Brien's prose. They
treated the film and the stories as if they were of the same medium, trans-
lating O'Brien's words into visual images. Reduced to a plotline, O'Brien's
vision does seem grim—a morbid caricature of lives not yet tethered to
the downward spiral of the finished stories. Placing themselves in the cir-
cumstances of O'Brien's characters, my students retained their sense of
autonomy; and they shrank from the frailty of characters who did not
exercise control over their lives the way they, the students, would. We can
easily imagine ourselves in another place; it is more difficult to imagine
being possessed of another consciousness.

Thinking about this discussion, I realize how often we talk about literature
in terms of its visual impact. "That would make a good movie," we say, as
if writing were merely raw material for a product Hollywood will varnish.
No wonder we are uncomfortable with language which resists reduction
to the visual.

Last term I offered another class the opportunity to skip one exam
if they could recite a hundred lines of verse from a class text. Only one

student took me up on it; she recited two poems perfectly, and when I asked her how she had done it, she said that she looked at the pages for so long that the print appeared before her mind's eye. Movies, print, television, music videos: it's not surprising that our society develops powerful visual imaginations.

But there is another kind of imagination, experienced not by sight but by listening. What's the difference between the imagination excited by visual stimuli and that other—what I'm calling here the "aural" imagination? For one thing, the visual affirms our sense that we are separate beings. We may wander real and imagined worlds, but however exotic the setting, we remain the same. We hear Marlow, but it is our own shadows steaming up the Congo; Huck drawls, but it is we who light out for the territory.

So the visual imagination inhibits us from experiencing something which literature as no other medium offers: the chance to be transformed, not just in space, but internally. "Poetry is the only art," says Galway Kinnell, "where what's inside us speaks, without medium of character, directly." I would extend his definition to include any literature which works through the avenues our society has least explored: the human voice, speaking.

Most societies have recognized that in imaginary traveling, the aural is vital. Shamans journeying to the other world *see* healing images but cannot bring them back. Instead, the shaman translates image into song: created in one world, heard in another. By relying solely on the visual imagination, we cut ourselves off from the rhythms that, even in the darkest fiction, offer healing, and in the happiest stories, remind us of mortality.

While my students may prefer the happy ending of *The Playboys,* I cannot believe the film will sustain them. As long as they *see* Tara, she remains discreet; she will not melt into their whispering consciousness. "Those who love the word serve it in action," writes Yeats. We put a premium on viewed action, but until we hear the internal voice, we remain deaf to the echoes of other voices doubling and deepening our own.

The tug and pull between the need to stay distinct and the desire to explode the walls which separate us provides a tension necessary to literary art. "Sadness was the form, happiness was the content," writes Milan Kundera in *The Unbearable Lightness of Being*. Kundera confronts the space between the form, revealed quite early in the novel (the lovers die in a traffic accident), and the secret happiness they share the night before they die. Perhaps this happiness can never be conveyed directly; perhaps the aural imagination is antithetical to direct statement. Still, however unknowable, this happiness radiates in the pleasure of language, delicate as the shell of the ear. Kundera's insight is equally true if turned around: "Happiness was the form; sadness was the content." Here the form is language, not fate; the content is mortality, not secret joy. We glimpse—or better, we hear— Lorca's *duende*—that ecstasy he felt in the presence of death.

"Have you heard the music that no fingers enter into?" asks Kabir. "Deep inside the soul—entangled music. / What is the sense of leaving your own house?" Until we have heard this entangled music, we will continue to scan horizons while staying stranded in our own skin. And this, it seems to me, is truly depressing.

O'Brien's stories engage us as intensely at the level of the musical phrase as at the level of plot and conception. To feel these stories, you have to hear them. You have to read them as medieval monks might have, moving their lips as their eyes scanned vellum; you must attend to the swellings and diminutions of tone that attest to the complexities the speakers express.

"Oh my dear I would like to be something else, anything else, an albatross," is how the speaker of "Over" plunges into her monologue:

> In short, I wish I never knew you. Or could forget. Or be a bone—you could suck it. Or a stone in the bottom of your pocket, slipped down, if you like, through one of the holes in the lining and wedged into the hem more or less forever, until you threw the coat away or gave it to one of your relations. I never saw you in a coat, only in a sort of jacket, what they call an anorak. A funny word.

Albatross, bone, stone, lining, hem, anorak—even in despair, we hear the music no fingers enter into, transmuting depression into grief.

The Scholar in the Hayfield

"A FREE house, free turf, and free milk; a root of standing corn, twelve drills of potatoes," crows Manus in *Translations*, Brian Friel's play about the colonization of Ireland in the 1840s.

"No, no, it's *rood*, not *root*," I think to myself, smiling. For this is a class production—though "production" is too grand a word. It's a one-night stand in the college pub on a makeshift stage under bar lights, attended by family, friends, and a few stray students who have dropped in for the first beer of the weekend.

"Manus," the lame scholar who tutors in his father's "hedge school," is played by John, a lithe young man in the last term, he hopes, of a BA program whose serpentine paths have dizzied the registrar. John is our "professional"; he works as a soundman for local rock bands at a nightclub where his cousin is a bouncer. The rest of the cast is on stage for the first time since they method-acted vegetables for the third grade pageant.

"Bridget" is a medical secretary back in school because the dentist she worked for retired; "Maire" is pregnant (though it's "don't ask/don't tell" right now); "Sarah" is a sophomore accounting major with a minor in education and a wrist tattoo; "Jimmy Jack" and "Doalty" are played—with some sleight of hand since the script calls for them to exchange a few lines of dialogue—by a wisp of a fellow whose quirky demeanor makes me think he might pull off this schizophrenic act; some days he seems as brilliant as "Jimmy Jack," the aged "Infant Prodigy," fluent in Greek and Latin; other days he's a convincing "Doalty Dan Doalty," with his hiccup and vapid stare. "Hugh," the schoolmaster, is played by a woman attending college along with her two grown children. On some rehearsal nights, her laughter has provided almost enough balm to make all this seem worthwhile.

As to how this performance came to be: it happened a bit like one of those old Mickey Rooney musicals, spontaneously combusting from a group moved by powers beyond their control. The idea was conceived at the end of a long class six weeks into the semester, when I asked, as if casually, how the term papers were going. From the freeze in the fidgeting, I could feel the group's dismay at the thought of actually writing the twenty-page papers called for in the syllabus. Until then we'd gotten along famously, playing our roles like old pros: students, professor. But that night it suddenly occurred to all of us that these roles required a performance we hadn't counted on: the production of term papers—something that threatened to upset the students' balancing act among school, work, and family, bringing our illusions crashing down on our heads.

This was my first time teaching Irish drama, and I panicked to think that even before midterm the props were coming apart. The term paper—a threat, downright blackmail, an exercise in failure—loomed ahead. To me it provided an assurance: as long as the normal amount of writing for a literature course was produced, as long as I wrote the usual comments and curved the usual grades, I could call the course a success. But that night, scanning their faces, I could see they were thinking that there just wasn't enough time for a term paper, what with all the costume changes their many roles required: workers, spouses, parents, students.

I realized, too, that I hadn't really been steering the course toward the goal of writing a paper. Yes, we'd critiqued the plays as literature; we'd discussed criticism; we'd chewed over sample paper topics. But somehow a feeling of complicity had seeped in, so that when I reminded them of the mission of the course, they felt vaguely betrayed.

The idea to skirt our way around this dolmen of a term paper had been planted innocently enough. I loved these plays: Yeats's "Noble Plays of Japan," O'Casey's Dublin Trilogy, Lady Gregory's folk-dramas, the lyric island plays of "that rooted man," J. M. Synge, as well as the contemporary works of Friel, Leonard, and Keane. We'd spent some class time reading aloud. How can anyone understand why the Dublin theatregoers pelted actors for saying "shift" without hearing the lines spoken? How can we understand Yeats's guilt, expressed in his famous lines, "Did that play of mine send out / Certain men the English shot," unless we hear the lines he feared started a war? So we'd tested our voices, bringing these plays briefly to life.

That night near Samhain at the end of a long class, John finally broke the awkward silence to suggest that maybe we could do something—anything—to make this cup pass away; perhaps we could even put on one of the plays we'd been reading instead of writing about them. I felt drawn to this little theatre company—no longer a class of computer-selected candidates for graduation, just a group of harried wayfarers—and my allegiance to the gods of curricula lapsed. Finally, with the giddy sensation of venial sin, I shrugged: "Why not?"

Of course in the weeks between that minor subversion and the night of the play, we repented many times. Neither they nor I had any idea how much time it took to prepare and stage a production. Even without set or costumes or choreography or elaborate stage directions, it turned out that a one-night stand demanded far more time than writing any term paper.

But throughout the laborious (and hilarious) rehearsals held in the pub after class, I could tell that although the play hadn't worked out as a time-saver, the students were glad to have undertaken it—partly for the pleasure of mastery and partly for the pleasure of getting away with something. Threaded through the chaos, I felt the group's thrill in taking control over one of the competing demands on their lives.

As much as we tout student empowerment, there can be no doubt that at an open-enrollment commuter school like Youngtown, the institution is a system, and a foreign one at that—as foreign as the English National Schools that are about to supplant the hedge schools in *Translations.*

Friel's play, set in the west of Ireland on the eve of the Famine, explores the uneven conflict between the dying Gaelic culture and the new order of the British Empire. Hugh's hedge school, a rustic vestige of an aristocratic tradition, offers Latin, Greek, even—"for the purposes of commerce"—a little English, in return for milk, moonshine, or whatever tuition the students can afford. As the first scene opens, Manus is preparing to teach class while outside, British sappers map out the small township of Beale Beag—or as it will soon be called, Bally Beg. They are making, as Captain Lancey says, "the first ever comprehensive survey of this entire country—a general triangulation which will embrace detailed hydrographic and topographic information and which will be executed to a scale of six inches to the English mile." What they are really doing, of course, is plotting the final phase of a conquest begun three hundred years before. As they anglicize names—Bun na hAbhann to Burnfoot; Druim Dubh to Black Ridge—they level the inner terrain, leaving the inhabitants with a choice: to move ahead toward "the landscape of fact," or to drift in an unmarked no-man's-land with no purchase on the future.

Just as Lancey proposes to erase local language and customs in the name of progress, so our university proposes to improve students' lives through education. We offer certificates and degrees; we boast the newest equipment; we shill financial aid; we promote outreach programs; we offer up-to-date training . . . And as our President says in the thirty-second spot aired at halftimes of our nationally televised football games, students here can "exceed their expectations." The locals wouldn't have it any other way. Everything we do is *good for them;* all our programs are designed with their needs in mind.

All this can be considered culturally neutral only if one thinks of the entire country as culturally homogeneous, as Lancey thinks of the British Empire. "This survey," the Captain says, "cannot but be received as proof of the disposition of this government to advance the interests of Ireland." But in Youngstown, as in Beale Beag, there are still traces of an indigenous culture, even if its presence has been overshadowed by the national culture. In fact, only thirty years ago Youngstown State was in essence a hedge school staffed by the community. In the seventies, in an attempt to increase enrollment and attract funding, the state replaced the locals with a slew of PhDs from around the country. Most of the local MAs were kept on as "limited service," just as Hugh hopes to hook on with the British National School that is to replace his hedge school.

Having arrived here in a later wave of that invasion, I owe my own job to the shift from hedge to National School. Nor is this the first time I've benefited. I once taught at the ultimate colonial site: the National University of

Zaire in Lubumbashi. My students came from the bush by foot, truck, boat, and train, to become Fulbright scholars and UN translators.

When I signed up with the Peace Corps, my MA sheepskin was still damp and I was schlepping lunch trays in an Atlantic City kosher restaurant. Within a month, I was lecturing Zairian grad students on the meaning of snow in "The Dead." Arriving in Africa, I felt immediately at home; and in this feeling I see now one of the paradoxes of colonization: having power makes you feel at home. Being welcome is a sign of having power. Frost puts it this way: "Home is the place where, when you have to go there, they have to take you in." In a colonial or postcolonial setting, that definition has a sinister ring.

Friel's play presents the conflict between cultures in terms of their competing assumptions. *Translations* is no paean to the Celtic Twilight. The play merely exposes the dynamic of colonization, and this dynamic, once set in motion, reveals how colonial encounters mold individuals into types. Certainly Lieutenant Yolland is such a type: feckless by his own admission, having landed in Ireland only because he missed the boat to another colonial destination, India. No one would consider Yolland powerful, neither politically nor personally, any more than I felt powerful bussing tables in Jersey; yet here in Bally Beg, Yolland feels inexplicably at home.

"The day I arrived in Bally Beg—no, Baile Beag—the moment you brought me in here, I had a curious sensation," Yolland says. "It was a momentary sense of discovery; no—not quite a sense of discovery—a sense of recognition, of confirmation of something I half knew instinctively." Yolland may not be a politically powerful Englishman, but English power has given him the freedom to explore his own psychic forces in a foreign landscape, and because he represents English power, the "natives" have to take him in, and he, like me, feels at home in a place to which he has no claim.

Friel's characters are each imprisoned in a different set of assumptions. What Lancey takes for granted is that the British Empire will define this place. Granting that, Hugh is certain that his own learning will protect him from the consequences of the transfer of power. Likewise, Hugh's prodigal son, Owen, now employed by the British as "civilian interpreter," assumes he can move gracefully between two worlds without being radically changed by one world or wholly forsaking the other. And what about my own assumption—that a course should be a course, bulwarked by a term paper? Even the word *course,* viewed under the scrutiny of the linguistic analysis of *Translations,* is shadowed by words like *racing, lines,* and something taken, *of course,* for granted.

Our production of *Translations* is made all the more comic by the fact that the character playing Owen has not been able to attend many rehearsals. He enters in possession of his first line but without resources after that. But this is no disaster: the rest of the cast prompt Owen in stage whispers, as if they are protected from view. Perhaps they are; perhaps they cannot be seen by anyone who brings to this stage an eye trained by the theatre of London and New York. Barely visible, the actors ignore foreign conventions like verisimilitude, in the same spirit that animates Doalty as he sneaks across the bog to shift the surveying machine planted by the British sappers. Doalty is merely—as they say in Ireland—"pulling the piss out of the Brits," but Manus recognizes the significance of the horseplay: "It was a gesture," he says; "Just to indicate . . . a presence."

The lines coaxed from an unprepared Owen are spoken just as Doalty and Bridget, following the script, conspire to cheat behind Hugh's back—because Hugh, as schoolmaster, also represents an authority worth subverting. The assumption in the hedge school seems much the same as my students' assumptions about stagecraft. Bridget and Doalty assume that Hugh's learning excludes from the daily interactions that take place so deep inside the culture that the idea of culture is not evident. Hugh's position is ambiguous: as an authority figure, he is feared, but as one of their own, he is needled playfully. "Three questions," jokes Doalty, mimicking the master's stilted Socratic style: "Question A—Am I drunk? Question B—Am I sober? (*Into* MAIRE'S *face) Responde—responde!*"

Just as the Greeks had no word for religion because it was so pervasive, Doalty and Bridget are so deeply immersed in their cultural assumptions that they take for granted the idea that maps and names are irrelevant to the unchanging rhythms of life. When the revolutionary "Donnelly twins" burn the soldier's camp, Bridget smells "the sweet smell" and fears not the vengeance of the British but only potato blight. When informed that the smell comes from an act of guerrilla warfare that will provide the excuse for the army to depopulate the region, she exclaims, "Ah Thank God, I thought we were destroyed altogether." So the whorls of culture, authority, subversion and play still revolve in the hedge school, a poignant contrast to the paternalism of colonial rule.

For the audience in the college pub, the irony is doubled: we know that the British are not fathers, and that their authority will extinguish the "children" they come to educate. We know that whether or not our actors perceive this course as rigorous, most of them will not gain from it the economic advantages they seek. This education can't be traded for anything. Like the students of Hugh's hedge school, my students will receive precious few economic benefits from their education. I meet graduates all the time: bartenders, mall workers, checkout clerks . . . No, getting a degree will not offer much advancement to most of these students.

The difference between my students and students at more prestigious universities is heightened for me this term because I'm teaching a course for the "Scholars," in a program for students selected by ACT scores and given full rides, taught in separate classes, and lodged in a special dorm. The attitude in this class is very different from that of my thespians. The Scholars want to know exactly what is expected of them from the first day, and their evaluation of the course is directly related to their sense of the appropriateness of the time allotted for it. Rather than work cooperatively, the Scholars are jealous of each other's grades, acutely aware of the competitive nature of the culture in which they aspire to excel.

While my undergraduates treat the university sometimes as a hedge school, sometimes a National School, to the Scholars (and to the state which replaced the local teachers with hired guns), it's very much a National School, and they support with vigor its "civilizing" purpose: teaching a foreign capitalist culture. Having accepted "the landscape of fact," the Scholars are here to succeed on terms which will separate them from their peers and families. Like Owen, and like the students they refer to as "Normal," the Scholars come for the most part from local working-class backgrounds, and—here is yet another level of irony—beyond their ken lies another class of students: children of professionals, akin to the class of Swift and Spenser, landed gentry who made their fortunes in Ireland but looked to London for cultural sustenance. You can be sure that the doctors' and lawyers' children—as well as the children of my own colleagues—will not attend our local state university, but will be sent "back East" for a pricy education.

Ultimately, the Scholars may find themselves in the same bind as Owen, the civilian interpreter whose attempt to identify with the new power proves futile. Like Owen—and like my would-be Fulbright scholars and UN translators at the National University of Zaire—these Scholars will have a difficult time entering the inner circles of power. In Ireland they are not British; in Africa, not white; and in contemporary America they don't have the pedigree.

Thinking about these Scholars, I realize that I am not like Hugh, though I occupy his position in this class. I have no claim of kinship with my students; they are not likely to cod me with mimicry. I come from New York, the son of Irish immigrants who believed so firmly in progress they wanted only to impel their offspring into a future defined by those they had fled.

While I identify with Hugh's avuncular bluster and find a strand of Yolland in my nostalgic memories of travel, it's the image of Owen which haunts me as I think about my relationship to this class. Like him, I hope to move blithely between worlds, translating what I know to be the inaccessible culture of the English into something palatable—a play. Certainly that was the way I was trained in the Peace Corps—playing at being native. How we strove to blend, to show that despite our jeans and radios and skin color, we were like our hosts: we ate their foods, we lived in their neighborhoods. We were very curious *msungus* indeed. It was as if we could pretend our American culture had not marked us, that we were here as newborns, ready to enter fully into the indigenous life. Even as we taught a new language and brought new technologies, we masked differences whose consequences none could escape. Perhaps, like Owen, I have pandered to these students by protecting them from "the landscape of fact." Perhaps I should have let them join me in making "a six inch map of the country." As Owen asks plaintively, "Is there something sinister in that?" Maybe not, but as Yolland reminds Owen, it is "an eviction of sorts." Owen himself finally comes to realize it is "a mistake—my mistake—nothing to do with us."

But watching the pleasure my students take in their tomfoolery, I wonder if some creative shadowboxing between cultures isn't taking place. If I find aspects of myself in Hugh, Yolland, and Owen, maybe my students can celebrate their resistance to "civilization" by adorning themselves for one night in some of its varied plumage. After all, *Translations* is a play in

English, the national language; it is a literary *objet* produced on Broadway; it is firmly wedged in the canon which colonization has sanctified, a colonization the play sets out to examine.

And tonight this play is theirs, offering provisional access to many identities; and the audience is theirs, won over by the unstinted energy of the spliced personae, by the Chaplinesque moustache sported by the cross-gendering Hugh, by the cheat sheets taped on the floor and the backs of chairs, by the video Maire's boyfriend is shooting, which we plan to show while we pull the piss out of each other at a cast party.

"Is it such a shameful thing to be born in Ireland?" St. Patrick once asked—himself a foreign emissary, the first Pax Corps Volunteer, who became, like so many colonizers and tourists after him, "more Irish than the Irish themselves." No, it is not a shameful thing, but it is a question only a foreigner could ask.

The danger in fantasizing a solidarity among different cultures is the usurpation of identities to which we have no honest claim. Likewise, romanticizing differences presents the danger of "remember[ing] everything," which as Hugh says, "is a form of madness." Throughout the last century, Romantic Twilights have darkened into pogroms. But our fantasy tonight is wound in the cloth of a play—it is not the only heart-sustenance: we remain multicultured, perhaps more aware of the many tributaries which enrich our blood. For an hour we are all players and watchers, colonizers and colonized. Though we are ultimately separated by the dynamics underlying *Translations,* tonight we are linked by the pageant, blessed with earnest work, laughter, and a curve-breaking, irrelevant, necklace of A's.

PART TWO

Curriculum for a Bardic School

By Heart

Curriculum for a Bardic School

I AM a bard. There, I've said it. Embarrassing, like wearing a sign saying "HUMBLE," or announcing you're a secret agent. Still, I have to come clean. Living in this country, in this era, is too trying. In Ireland it was no big deal. You could recite the length of your arm and not be bothered. I once heard a woman in a Donegal pub do the entire Molly Bloom soliloquy impromptu, right down to her knickers, and the two bogmen in the snug never unclenched their pipes. And in Africa, teaching in the then province of Katanga in the then nation of Zaire, what with no books anyway and fidgety lightbulbs, reciting poems was just passing on the news, as well as a way to ward off snakes on the walk home. But in the United States, we leave singing to the pros. When I toss my head back and take flight, I'm seen as a ham, or an autist who might be useful counting cards, or a Lothario, or a compulsive. Then there are the gobshites exclaiming, "How do you remember all that?" And last week a guy in a suit slipped me a buck.

I never intended to become a bard, even if I was a fey child. "A.D.D."—they'd call it now. Between serving Latin mass and rocking in front of the hi-fi absorbing the family collection of Clancy Brother albums, I was immersed in mysterious language from the age most children take up reason. But being a bard is not the kind of vocation even a strange child aims for. There's no counseling, no pie charts. The profession is badly marketed, completely misunderstood. Shakespeare did a terrible disservice, or more likely it wasn't Shakespeare himself, but the bards—real ones—who came after. Shakespeare was no bard. He broke the cardinal rule: he became famous.

I'm not a bard like that—with a capital letter and a prophet's beard and a college named after him. I'm from a school created before nuns or whisky. We're teaching poets, beneath the high fili, who created the riddling rosc poetry—more obscure than Pound. The fili were ex-druids who loved sex too much to become monks, I think. Though word is the monks didn't do badly.

I've come forward now because I'm tired of all the whining. Everyone's complaining about the state of the art. There's no money in it. No one reads poetry. Universities have cloistered the great voices. Grim-faced essays take the patient's temperature, and there's even a book, *Can Poetry Matter?*, which pronounces the situation almost hopeless.

So I thought now might be the time to write down a few things I've heard, because when you know about bards, you'll know that the fellow stuttered when he framed his question. It's not *Can*, Mr. Gioia; it's *Is*. *Is* poetry matter. Is it good for you like broccoli or prose?

Bards take the matter out of poetry, take it off the page, away from the publishers and pundits, out of the libraries and cafe-conglomerate bookstores, and lodge it in memory, where many voices blend. Voiced, the poem is transfigured from a printed glyph to sensory language: ephemeral, but with a tensile strength derived from the collective memory that births it. Critics may feel differently, but what matters to a poem is not how many times it is reprinted, but how deeply it penetrates the heart.

The proliferation of bad poetry seems to frighten critics more than the prospect of steady labor. Maybe they're afraid that in such numbers not all the poems written can be stamped, and a few bad ones might get through and be mistaken for good ones, and then the ivy shivers. To grease the hand-wringing, I can only think of what one bard whose name I won't betray told us.

"I've got some good news and some bad news," he said. "The bad news is that 90 percent of the poetry you read is going to be dreck. The good news is that the 10 percent left over is enough to last three lifetimes."

What better way to filter out the dreck than to start learning the 10 percent by heart?

Learn by heart, I say. Not *memorize.* I am not a minstrel, not a professional performer. There's more to being a bard than memorizing. Memorizing is an act of will, but learning by heart is capricious. Minstrels memorize what they are paid to learn, so their performance is not a tribute to the poem. The heart doesn't enter in. They're lovely to hear, minstrels are, but they do no more than sing for their supper, which is why in the old days they were consigned to sit furthest from the fire with the mercenaries. Now, of course, they own castles.

There are stages in learning a poem by heart. The first is finding it. The best way to find a poem is to hear it in the voice of another bard. The experience can be so powerful that you learn the poem almost immediately; it brands itself into memory, and you can hardly remember a time you didn't know it. Hearing James Wright recite Thomas MacDonough's translation of Cathal Buidhe MacGilla Gunna's poem "An Bannan Bui" was like that for me. I can hardly resist it now: "The Yellow Bittern that never broke out in a drinking bout might as well have drunk..." But it's not the same. I haven't the heart for it on the page.

You might ask why I drop Wright's name when I shielded the other. That's part of the tradition: when identities mingle, as Wright's and MacDonough's and Cathal Bui's do, names blend in a minor chord. You might feel this harmony when you hear a poem and find that in the one hearing it has become yours, as if you wrote it. Your identity and that of the poet blur, becoming irrelevant. I think of Robert Bly's translation of Kabir: "this is what love is like: suppose you had to cut your head off / and give it to someone else, / what difference would that make?"

Most people don't believe such a thing could happen to them. They think they'd have to do a St. Paul to learn a poem by heart after one hearing. But it's not a conversion experience. In bars and classrooms I've shown drunks and third graders how to do it. The poem I use most often to give people the experience of learning a poem in one hearing is a well-worn Renaissance piece, so finely harmonized that it's anonymous. It's called "The Man of Double-Deed," and if you'd like to try your heart at

learning, give this book to someone right now and have them read the
poem aloud, once.

> There was a man of double deed,
> who sowed his garden full of seed.
> When the seed began to grow,
> twas like a garden full of snow.
> When the snow began to fall,
> like birds it was upon the wall.
> When the birds began to fly,
> twas like a shipwreck in the sky.
> When the sky began to crack,
> twas like a stick upon my back.
> When my back began to smart,
> twas like a penknife in my heart.
> And when my heart began to bleed,
> then I was dead and dead indeed.

Sometimes a poem doesn't take your breath away on a first hearing or
you never hear the poem in the first place. Instead you find it on the page.
There's another kind of pleasure, akin to mature love, in learning by heart
a poem you've never heard spoken. You can compose the music of the
poem in your own voice. Even if you don't have the excitement of a first
hearing, you begin to feel after a while which poems need to be remem-
bered. Whitman still soars, as does Williams and a surprising amount of
Pound. Eliot, poor soul, can't flutter. But this is all bard room quarreling.
You'll recognize the poems your memory yearns for.

Lift the poem off the page carefully, and don't strain to hold it aloft too
long. I once visited the workroom of a bard in Wales (I might as well admit
it's Dylan Thomas—I can't shield a bard that big). Tourists filed past the
shack on the banks of the Larne where Thomas worked, preserved just as
it was before the White Horse. On the table was a tablet of handwritten
poems—not his own, but Yeats, Herrick, Pope. I didn't have to be told
what he was up to. He was lifting the poems off the pages of books and
placing them down again in his own hand, leaving a diaphanous imprint
on memory. Do it a few times till your thumb aches. Then you're ready for
the next stage, which is to take the poem walking.

While learning a poem after one hearing feels like inspiration, learning a poem line by line while walking in its rhythms is as close as a bard gets to the miracle of composition reserved for the fili. Words tease, vanish, then reappear from nowhere. Paroled from the page, a poem might even reveal its source out in the open air. It's a strange experience. For one thing, if you're used to reading, your head's tilted differently. It takes some getting used to, seeing the sky, the trees, the fields—the very fabric of the poem— while immersed in a word-hoard. Don't trip.

Something happens when a line is being lifted for the last time from the sheet in your hand to its new and ancient home in memory. You feel the rhythm linking synapses that haven't before touched, redrawing memory's map, becoming yours. Afterwards, a tinge of that first walking might linger with the poem; years later you might glimpse a maple tree or a cloud sheering sunlight or a '69 Impala and you'll be set off: "Vowels plowed into other, open ground." Or: "I cannot think of anything today that I would rather do." Or: "Two evils, absent, either one apart." No earthly reason at all.

When you have a sheaf of poems by heart, that's it. You're a bard. There's no degree, no laurels. I hope you won't be as foolish as I've been about announcing it. I know you won't. If there were a school for bards, I'd offer this curriculum. Courses can be repeated over and over.

Curriculum for a Bardic School

Have by heart at least five poems for any ceremony.

Have by heart poems for all occasions, including eating oysters, walking in the autumn leaves, dancing naked in the house; but more important, have the grace to know when reciting will augment these occasions, and when it will sully them.

Sing with passion and without skill.

Have by heart poems too long or strange to tell others: poems you recite to yourself falling asleep or on long plane trips.

Never say you know a poem till you know it by heart.

Know a poem by each of your friends, even the friends who spoke theirs by accident.

Know poems by people you don't like, as a reminder the muse is no priest.

Partake in the flow of language, taking almost as much pleasure from finding a poem as making one.

Never borrow or lend books of poetry; always buy and give them away. Buying commits you to commit a poem to memory. Giving away affirms that you have done so.

Spend more money on books than any other item without a motor or roof.

Spend more time learning poems than reading them.

Find one book which you treat the way the ancients treated the Bible, the *Uphanishads,* the *Táin Bó Cúailnge,* the *Neibelungenlied,* the *Epic of Gilgamesh,* the Koran. Read it as if it were the only book you'll ever read.

Never finish a book of poems without committing to learn a poem by heart. If the book doesn't have a poem to learn, don't finish it.

Beware applause. Ask yourself, Who are they clapping for, Ace? If they're clapping for you, they've missed the poem. If they're clapping for the poet—well, that's a bit like clapping in a movie theatre.

Beware audiences over a hundred. Spoken poetry must be felt by the bard as well as by the listeners, and each listener uses up some part of the necessary feeling. Why a hundred? Because Yeats says a hundred.

Don't use poems as parlor tricks.

Never let someone else choose the poems you learn by heart. Accept no penance.

As much as I might like to christen a bardic school with all the trappings, it needs to be said that memory should never be held like a bludgeon over the page-bound. The oral tradition has its tyrannies. For one thing, it's hard not to learn by heart poems which seem to have been written with an audience in mind. The heart yearns for wholeness, and naturally chooses poems with a skin. Fragments of many states of mind—these are less memorable, but equally valuable. It is important not to rely only on the dramatic poems.

Poetry is not only, as somebody (I forget who) said, "memorable speech"; it is also the most forgettable speech. Unmoored by plot or character, its lack of reference can make for difficult remembering. This is especially true in the last century, when the mnemonic devices have become passé. Some poetry seems to be written expressly to prevent remembering. I defy his own mother to recite a hundred lines of Zukovsky, though *A* remains unparalleled, if unread. Sometimes I can open a book I've read and not remember a single poem, though it may be a fine book indeed.

The yearning toward the unsayable extends beyond what even the bardic memory can hold. They were always the fili's gifts and they still are. Perhaps being a bard is no longer a healthy, full-time occupation. Maybe in this millennium we need to forget as well as remember. So it can be useful to try your heart in another way: see if perhaps you're not a fili. The experience of failing at something grand is never wasted. Who knows? You might find your words sung one day by some Homer. Now there was a bard. Pity they put a name on him.

The Sea Is Wild Tonight

A Pilgrimage to Ancient MFAs

ON THE westernmost ledge of Europe, near Slea Head in the Kingdom of Kerry, huts of corbelled stone cluster by the Atlantic. Clocháns, they are called, quarried from native rock and hefted into place a thousand years ago, though a thousand years means little to these sea-sprayed fields. If not for the hand-printed sign advertising, "Dunbeg Stone Fort—Beehive Huts Ahead," I might have trundled past, having my hands full keeping my rental from careening into gorgeous oblivion. I unfold my Yankee length from the sedan and rattle the chain until a pensioner in burdocked overalls shambles down the path to unlock the gate and collect the two euro admission. As we climb gorse hillocks, he keeps up a hum of badinage about Skellig Michael and the Book of the Dun Cow, along with Kevin and Colmcille and the Blind O'Driscolls, as if raillery could coax them back to life.

"Where's home?" he asks; then mulls "Ohio" knowingly, as if to seal the secret. At the crest of a mound, he stiffens a finger at the dense, silent city of beehive huts.

They are eight flint humps rising from packed clay. I circle them, then lean against the largest, patting its warty flank. Somehow, with no moldings or wood supports, the makers have executed a mousehole-shaped doorway. I peer into the thigh-high portal, then bend deeper to enter the dark. Inside, moss and clay close in. As my eyes adjust, flecks of daylight pierce the unmortared stone.

Reemerging into light that now seems brilliant, I wonder who lived here. I don't know much about eighth-century architecture, but it's clear that more commodious hovels could have been dug, even out of straw. And there was wood here once, before the forests were cleared.

"Twas the poets," crows our host, with a look that seems to mock an age that mistakes height for stature.

As he expounds on the annals of this desolate place, rhapsodizing about bards who memorized thousands of lines and fili who encoded the esoteric rosc poetry—"the like of which wasn't heard again until that Joyce fella"—it dawns on me that these were early MFAs. Our guide doesn't know the exact requirements, but the curriculum, he says, took between twelve and twenty years to complete, depending on the degree. There were brehons, a class of poet-lawyers who could splice royal lineages as far back as Finn MacCumhal, and monks who cribbed a hunk of Western Civ on moldy vellum. Behind the monks lurked the specter of druids, whose secret examinations were so perilous that only one in three survived.

Well, between the ritual deaths and the frigid dorms, the registrar wouldn't have been too busy.

It's a commonplace to say that MFA programs produce too many writers. Asked if writing programs didn't wind up discouraging young writers, Flannery O'Connor famously replied: "not nearly enough." But it seems an odd complaint. After all, what's wrong with breeding talent? Ancient cultures set aside resources for artistic training; why shouldn't we? And while we're at it, why not pipe in some heat and cut a skylight?

Over the last half-century, MFA programs have allowed generations of students from diverse backgrounds to cultivate their gifts. Even if most of our graduates don't wind up on *Oprah,* they will have experienced an apprenticeship in a mind-broadening field; they will have learned principles of form and nuance that translate into many occupations, and they will have plumbed their potential for self- and world-awareness. At the very least, they will have become better readers.

Thus preaches my committee in Ohio, and thus have we held during the long years of shaping a new consortial MFA program among a cluster of four state universities, each encrusted with a bureaucracy as hermetic as these huts. Appealing for the benediction of the Board of Regents, we spaded proposals, chiseled curricula, and spread spreadsheets over round-tables like fresh straw. The campaign took as long as it once took to certify a bard.

One document we had no trouble composing was the "Needs State-ment." Having viewed the dizzy graphs, we knew that there'd be plenty of applicants. In Northeast Ohio, just as across the country, the workshops are filling up.

We had a bit more of a problem when it came to explaining what we thought all these students would do after they graduate. They could teach, of course; and we put that down right away. Numero Uno. But a glance at current classes—one prof for fifteen students—revealed that none but a few would achieve this august goal. PhDs are in the same boat: they sur-vive at about the same rate as wannabe druids. What fraction of our grads climbs on the tenure track? The graphs didn't say.

Without certification they can't teach in public high schools, but they might hook up with Poets in the Schools programs, or join the swelling army of adjuncts, or coach soccer at prep school. But even jerry-rigged, the ark leaked. So we needed another plank. And we found one:

> While the MFA is not a vocational degree, creative writing and publish-ing constitute a large enterprise that requires new talent.... Major companies in Northeast Ohio depend on a supply of skilled writers and editors. The internship collaboration with local communities, as well as the teaching experience available to MFA teaching assistants, will equip our graduates to enter new and expanding writing fields.

Fair enough. The world needs editors, technical writers, advertisers; and the MFA degree offers an ideal preparation for all sorts of writing, just as the committee claims. But today, with the whitecaps mounting coastal granite and the wind stinging the wildness into a wet squint, it all seems awfully tame. I think of a tenth-century poem scrawled by a monk in the margins of his calligraphy, written in a stone settlement just like this one.

> The sea is wild tonight.
> No need to fear

that Viking hoards will come
and terrify me.

Do I envy that ancient poet scanning the Atlantic through a chink in his beehive hut? He faced no committees, no boards. No need to justify his scarecrow muse. But I don't yearn to take his place. I'd miss the food and company and light and warmth—and those Vikings sound more dangerous than a provost. Yet today I could almost yield to the conceit that even in Ohio we live on the edge of a great ocean, peering into the mist, the way these ancient hut dwellers did. The sea is not the Atlantic with its terrifying ships, and our universities are far from beehive huts. They are capacious, Starbucked, crackling with Wi-Fi. In fact, they seem more like great longships themselves, raiding coasts the Vikings never dreamt of.

And what, to stretch this metaphor, do they raid? Why do these splendid vessels terrify?

Drenched and stiff-limbed, I think with tenderness of the rolling seas of Ohio. I'm proud of the work that my colleagues and I did conceiving, planning and implementing the NEOMFA program. From four separate entities we made a web. We forged bonds among our faculties and paved the way for a program with a virtual campus encompassing hundreds of square miles. We fostered a community that crisscrosses the rust belt. We've even laughed about getting a school bus. Still, I feel uneasy. I can't speak for my colleagues, but in all our meetings I never felt truly at home. I never wrote or spoke in my own language, never thought about the wayward accidents that had nourished my own writing life or how to bring them to bear on younger lives. Not that I want to inscribe our proposal on parchment, or chant it in rosc, or storm the Regents, proclaiming like Cuchulain, "I give no more proof than the hawk gives that he's no dove." But as I recall our solid, serviceable, and successful proposal, with its headings and subheadings and graphs and samples, I wish that somewhere in the margin I had doodled: "the sea is wild tonight / No need to fear . . ."

What I feared then was abandonment. If we didn't sell our program in terms administrators would approve, we would not be allowed a seat on the great ship. What I fear now, after we've been ushered on board, is that in composing a plan shaped by the university's priorities, we tainted something essential at the core of creativity. It might be something felt only in the dark, when even the chinks of light fade.

I fear, even more than slashed budgets and fainting enrollment, being absorbed by a culture that tolerates but does not sustain us. I fear that in defining ourselves in foreign terms like "accountability," "progress," and "utility," we forsake the place where we are most useful, accountable to the voices that speak through us from the past. I fear that in gaining a chair at the amply set table, we lose our way back to a grave darkness that, once extinguished, may be beyond recovery.

How would such a self-fulfilling proposal look? What would I change, after a pilgrimage to these ancestral MFAs? It's tempting to say I'd fling the doors open to artists and performers and visionaries and yes, even lawyers—if they were bold enough to enter a world without codicils. I'd ask students to choose an authentic art using the tools most native: sound, memory, insight, or vision. Writing is not the only way to find this place; it's just a technology, and should not rule by fetishistic power. Of course we'd have no poetry majors, fiction majors, creative nonfiction majors, translation majors, or playwriting majors. Erase the boundaries. Instead of huddling them into genres, let specialties emerge and entwine out of immersion in all. Modern descendants of early MFAs should know that they have more in common with the motley inhabitants of this silent city than with people who make advertisements, or write briefs, or edit newspapers—or draft university proposals. Open the workshops. But close the craft and theory courses: veil the mysteries from all but initiates. For internships let's have real ships. Require penniless travel and field work in pastures instead of offices. Teach work that pays the rent, engages hand and mind and frees us from selling genius to a market which twists talent to its own ends. Give credit to poems that bring rain—or, in this climate, stop it. Credit for stories that sift into the underworld. Credit for not writing sequels. Graduation comes at the point of exhaustion or death or a reentry into selfhood that bears the world inside. Yes, it's tempting, in the slanting rain as I trudge back to my car from a hillock near Slea Head, to revise our MFA proposal. But I don't want these changes, except in dreams where Ohio is a stormy coast. With my colleagues at home, I stand by the words we wrote.

But I want a larger space for such dreams. Or should I say—after squeezing into a beehive hut—a more intense space, so real and present that it might tint the fluorescent light of a committee room or throb in the engine of an old beater bearing a student across the whaleroad of Northeast Ohio. Let this small dark space remind us who we are, where we come from, and what, if we fail to dream, we might become.

Autenticité

IT'S GREEN. Fern, myrtle, chartreuse, Platonic-Kelly. Shamrock-on-steroids. And it's everywhere: derbies, balloons, twirlers, buttons, sneakers, bunting, vests, glitter, boutonnières, smoke. On the limelit stage, the band cranks up. The lead singer sports spiky hair and a harlequin kilt. The tin whistler's jeans are spray-painted K.M.R.I.A. (he must be the English major—it's Joycean for "Kiss My Royal Irish Arse"). Tonight is the high holy moneymaker and they're making the most of it, crooning and ululating and diddlydydaying. Right now they're deep into a Guinness book–length medley of *It's No Nay Ireland Says The Wild Colonial Unicorn's Galway Danny Where It's A Long Way To Mother Macree And Has Anybody Here Seen My Wild Irish Rose*—nuggets of such dreck they must have spilled out of a date-expired box of Lucky Charms. The emerald mob congeals to climax, chorusing that old Irish tune, "Gilligan's Island." Wild applause.

Did anybody ever think any of this was good? Were any of these tunes once hummed on an April afternoon by a gossoon hiking the twelve miles from Cavan Town on the road to Killeshandra? If so, by what process were they strained of flavor and nuance, and injected, like the flu, into the aesthetic arteries of an entire population? If this sexless bacchanalia represents an invocation, what is it calling for? If it's a ritual, what does it reenact? What is it we yearn for?

Right now I can relate to one particular yearning—to be anywhere else. Maybe that's how it begins. Growing up in Flushing, which my parents pronounced "Sligo," our theme song was "Everybody Knows This is Nowhere." The row houses, the triple-digited streets, the plastic Pegasus gas stations, the unpithed hearts and TV dinners, all seemed proof that only by fictive flight could we propel ourselves toward a home that was not completely sanitized of meaning. For me, that fantasy came to life one Saturday morning as I thumbed through the remainder rack of LPs in Korvettes' emporium. Amid the mind-blowing covers of Iron Butterfly, Procol Harem, and Jethro Tull was an album featuring four men in white sweaters in front of a canvas backdrop. There it was, the place I didn't come from, where I wasn't born and raised, where I knew no one: Home.

I wedged that LP into the cabinet hi-fi and played it raw. Afternoons at a time, I rocked on hands and haunches, back and forth, speed adjusted to song.

My father would roll his eyes and say, "Up the Rebels."

My mother hissed back, "Narrowback!"

With money shaved from lunch I collected the entire Clancy Brothers and Tommy Makem opus: *Hearty & Hellish; Isn't It Grand, Boys; The Boys Won't Leave the Girls Alone; The First Hurrah; Home, Boys, Home*—along with Paddy Noonan, The Dubliners, The Irish Rovers, The Merry Ploughboy.

I listened so hard I believed I understood the words: moonshine, porter, poteen and sassanach made sense. I was langers; peelers, pishogues and fenians harried and cocked; I roved; I stood and delivered—a bloody briny daft shoneen with an eye peeled for a crubeen or a colleen, a dragoon, an amadon, a quay.

Soon I began to understand Gaelic and *ad fiason la port laragot, fa dow, fa dee, fa le god-e-lum* was clear to me as *with houls ime shoos ame tows peepin troo siyin shinnymarinkadootaloffin ould jonny doo.*

In third grade, I became the ambassador of fantasy—plucked by Sr. Miriam Eileen out of the back row and ushered into the sixth grade to preen like an exotic bird and croak "O'Donnell Abu" to the apprentice thugs and prom queens. Though I hewed strictly to routine, walking straight home after school to boil franks with Dinty Moore and watch

"Speed Racer," I lived in a phantasmagoria of faeries, warriors, wild geese, turf fires, and bathos. I mimed step dances. I named our dog "Wolfe Tone." I said Gaelic Mass in my bedroom with a tissue box tabernacle and bathrobe vestments while Wolfe served as acolyte. My mother thought I'd had a stroke when she saw my fourth-grade school picture because I'd curled my lip in what I took for an Irish smile. Life sailed on between Innisfree and Flushing until fifth grade when the Masterson twins from Limerick enrolled. If they looked like a pair of snivelers who didn't know a bunt from a burrito, they were certifiably more Irish than I was. I never got the nerve even to say hello.

The desire to be somewhere authentic without moving isn't limited to children, or once-a-year-Paddies, or the denizens of faceless suburbs. I've seen a whole country overwhelmed. The flag was green there too—olive drab, with a jaundiced circle into which a black arm thrust a torch. Painted on walls, flying above office buildings, stenciled on T-shirts, it was omnipresent. Where you didn't see the pennant, you saw the portrait of the man behind it, wearing a leopard-skin hat and gripping a tribal staff. He'd changed his name from Joseph Mobutu to Mobutu Sese Seko Kuku Benza Waza Banga (Mobutu, He Himself, The Cock That Fears No One). He was President for Life and Father of the Nation. When the Katanga province revolted, he renamed it Shaba. He transformed his native village into an animist shrine. He rechristened the entire country, thwarting cartographers by replacing "The Congo"—on account of its colonial taint—with "Zaire," a word with no definitive history, though some said it came from a Portuguese mispronunciation of the Congolese word for "river." He forbad cravats, preferring Nehru-style abacosts. Political rallies featured drumbeat-driven dances performed by women wearing pagnes silkscreened with the leader's portrait. *Autenticité,* he called it, implying that the war-torn, impoverished country which the "Zairois" experienced every day was merely a façade. If Mobutu's vision was a figment, it was less elusive than his nation's bounty, sequestered in the President's Swiss bank account.

While *autenticité* usually tints the present through the lens of a monochromatic past, sometimes it peers into the future. Describing communist Czechoslovakia, Milan Kundera links programmatic political thought with a cultural aesthetic he calls "kitsch." Kundera's kitsch results from an effort to cleanse; it is, as he says, "a categorical renunciation of shit." Every institution has its kitsch, he contends: there's communist kitsch, capitalist kitsch, Christian kitsch and even perhaps Buddhist kitsch.

Kitsch, or *autenticité*, or merely sentimentality: all renounce the messy, the frayed, the unclean. But I wonder if there isn't more. Maybe the desire for *autenticité* emerges from a dissatisfaction with the here and now—that prison from which none escape, and from which we seem eternally excluded. When the kaleidoscope of this absent-present makes us dizzy, we shut our eyes tight and envision some Edenic past or utopian future, even though the squint turns everything green or red. Depending on how you spin the palette, it's not that far perhaps from Flushing to Zaire to the Communist bloc to the *autenticité* of the Third Reich or of Bush's America, where demagogues have rallied millions in the name of a fantastic past and future.

Easy now, boy. Take a sip. I can't get all wound up. After all, I'm not merely a spectator here at this St. Patrick's Day free-for-all in Youngstown, Ohio—itself a Hittite anagram for "nowhere." My band's up next.

Yes, despite the Masterson setback, I find myself propped once again in front of overgrown sixth-graders to flog the ould songs. We've been at it for years, and it's great *craic*. Living rooms, bars, churches, auditoriums, parking lots, theatres, and festivals: we've hit all the hot spots of Northeast Ohio and beyond. Not to mention the occasional livening up of a moribund faculty reception. But tonight's different. After watching the first band cudgel the crowd into a frenzy, my bandmates eye me warily. It won't be original ballads or poems set to music or jazzed up arrangements tonight—not with this crowd, not on your life. Nothing but schlock will do. And I'm a veritable jukebox of schlock.

The prospect of reliving my own version of *autenticité* highlights the contrast between tonight's gig and the tunes we play on the other 364. In fact, sometimes I wonder if we're an Irish band at all. My fellow band members come from very different angles altogether. There's Jim Andrews, a physicist; Kelly Bancroft, a fiction writer; Will Greenway, the poet laureate of Georgia; and Istvan Homner, a Transylvanian mandolin player. Not a green strand in the helix. And what about our long-haired musical leader and composer, Steve Reese, who also "digs with the other foot," as they say in Flushing?

When I imagine Steve Reese's childhood, I think of a different kind of *autenticité* altogether. He grew up in Ithaca, in the Finger Lake District of upstate New York—a hamlet, as it appears from the greenish distance of time and envy, of steeples, ivy, antique shops and cafes. Set in a valley between two campuses, it is replete with presentness, nearly living up to its Homeric etymology as a byword for home. While I was bussing around meadowless Fresh Meadows, waterless Bayside and dystopian Utopia, Steve Reese biked home from his red-bricked, white-columned schoolhouse down Cayuga Street, named after the local tribe, onto Willow Ave, lined with real willows. Arriving at a home that must have been Dutch Colonial, he too was immersed in music. But there was no autistic bobbing on threadbare carpet (a practice which, by the way, has had the collateral effect of fitting me perfectly for the bodhrán). Instead, Steve Reese learned to play a guitar his brother had handcrafted. The Reese brothers hunched over reel-to-reel recordings of James Taylor, Dylan, Joan Baez, and a thousand other troubadours, slowing the tape down to amplify each lick until they had absorbed a quadrant of the airwaves. Reese honed his gift playing in country and rock bands while grinding out an Eng. Lit. PhD at the University of Delaware, where by strange fortune our paths almost crossed—Steve arriving just after I lit out from Blue Hen country for Zaire and *autenticité*.

Late at night, buttery with whisky, our rehearsals often melt into a songfest from those days, as Steve rocks through unholy medleys—everything from "Take a Letter Maria" and "The Inessential Woody Guthrie" to "Dead Skunk in the Middle of the Road." He has a chunk of Americana by heart, making up for everything I missed.

His solo album, *The Feast of St. Monday,* is an eclectic blend of ballads and alternative rock. Reese's homemade guitar speaks like a lucid voice, textured with fiddle, bass, and drums, and there's not a song on the CD whose lyrics wouldn't stand on their own as spoken poetry. But as much as I love *The Feast of St. Monday,* the work he's done with the band is, for me, the thing I can't account for.

It's wildly inauthentic. Reese clamps some electric chords on James Clarence Mangan's "Rest Only in the Grave" with enough juice to jolt J.C.'s liver back to life, and restore bits of Davis and Ferguson too.

He's added a stave to that bottomless barrel of whisky encomiums (matched in number only by curses spit at the same commodity) by composing a paean that goes both ways. Each verse, in claiming how "the whisky rescued me," savors the misery it renounces. "For love no man I've met is fit / Long of wind and dim of wit," sings Kelly, our lead soloist (and for those on the inside, the irony's tarter since Steve's her husband). Kelly's quip, like the other stanzas, featuring unrequited love (Steve), poverty (moi), and loneliness (our happily married physicist) is punctuated by a harmonic toast: "A drink before I leave this world," and "A drink before I go." It's the only drinking song I know that curses what it praises.

More ambitious still, "Heart of the Stranger" draws from Walt Whitman's *Specimen Days* to relive an encounter with an Irish soldier who came to America "to fight for Lincoln in '63." Midway through, the melody yields to a spoken stanza of Whitman's "Reconciliation," mediating song and speech, documentation and interpretation. Because the Whitman-esque refrain, "Little he knew, poor death stricken boy, / The heart of the stranger that hovered near," reveals the sensibility embodied in all these songs, *Heart of the Stranger* became the title of our second CD.

Another composition mixes the structure of a contemporary alternative song, including bridge, refrains, harmonies, and dueling instrumental breaks, with lyrics that echo the testimonial narratives of nineteenth century sheet ballads. The result brings to life the voice of a woman about to board one of the infamous Famine Ships:

> In the end we'd grown desperate,
> Having for our only meal,
> A handful of Peel's brimstone,
> And whatever we could steal.

> My husband left us at the workhouse door,
> And the child growing weak,
> I staggered the road down to Dublin,
> The famine ships to seek.

Unable to completely extinguish his academic instincts, Prof Reese has nosed through many volumes to uncover elements that seldom reach contemporary ballads. Peel's brimstone, for instance, refers to the indigestible grain that Sir Robert "Orange" Peel imported to feed the starving

Irish. Likewise, Reese links nodes of oppression, observing that "The boat smelled of sugar and molasses / From its West Indies port of call." Personal and immediate, the suffering evoked by "Famine Ship" ripples far beyond national borders.

Then there's the blues number laid on the fourteenth century Welsh poet, Dafydd ap Gwilym. Opening with a bass riff that Dafydd's descendant, Muddy Waters, might have jammed, Reese wails:

> A plague upon the women of this parish.
> What's wrong that they don't want me.
> Not just the girls, but the wives and widows.
> It's unnatural; it's villainy.

"Dafydd's Lament" moderates a quarrel between the poet and his accusers, who respond in a lighter modality: "To lie between a maiden's legs is the one thing on his mind. / In his eyes the fire of lust is all that you will find." When the women finish flaying the arse off him, the instrumentals descend back into the blues to preface the next chapter from the aging poet.

The inventiveness of this hybrid becomes more apparent if we peek backstage at some sources. Here's a sample, translated in *The Celtic Poets*:

> Furious and indignant am I!
> A plague on the women of this parish,
> For I never had one of them, ever
> Nothing but failed endeavor,
> Not a prayer with a tender maid,
> Nor girl, or wife or hag!

Not hard to see the grain Reese works against: the stilted "furious," "indignant," "endeavor," and "never had I one." Yet, in unvarnishing Dafydd's lust, Reese hasn't merely sanded down the diction—this is no Beat version. "Plague," "parish," "unnatural," and most delicious of all, "villainy," ink the colloquial lines with a kind of medieval slang.

Unlike the first-person lyric format of the translations in *The Celtic Poets,* "Dafydd's Lament" reframes an ancient practice: the poetic contest. Such sparring tournaments have ancient roots; they provide the template for Oedipus's riddling; and they appear in many medieval poems, perhaps most famously in Brian Merriman's bawdy *The Midnight Court,* where early feminists put the male gender on trial, deciding we come up (cough) short. Such contests are frequently featured in rap, and "Dafydd's Lament" incorporates a strand of this genre by devolving into a spoken brawl: "Look at him with his oily eyes; more white hair than my grand-mother," say the women; to which the poet can only pluck a G and splut-ter, "Oh, it's unnatural."

Reese digs further back into the canon to give voice to "The Old Woman of Beare," an anonymous eighth century Irish poem. Again, it's instructive to see the material from which his lyrics are culled. Here's a stanza from *The Faber Book of Irish Verse:*

> Ebb tide has come for me:
> My life drifts downwards
> Like a retreating sea
> With no tidal turn.

This postmodernist translation bends the slant rhymes of Gaelic verse into jagged lines. Reese takes the simple tone, along with more fulsome treatments by Frank O'Connor and Kuno Meyer, and gives the poem a new spin, based on a 3/4 time signature that syncopates accented and slant rhymes against a complex melodic pattern:

> The sea it crawls away from shore,
> Leaves weeds like a corpse's hair.
> That desolate, withdrawing sea is in me,
> I'm the old woman of Beare . . .

Of course, exegesis can't convey the pleasure of sitting around my living room, as we did last night, encircled by vocal harmonies, two guitars, man-dolin, bass, and bodhrán, knowing that this place in rainy March in Ohio is the only spot on earth where this eighth century poem is being played in the spirit that ensorcelled the windwracked Beare peninsula 1200 years ago. Last night, it felt palpable: the tensile strength that comes from the melding of influences.

Often, popular music erases any trace of absence, insisting, in an inversion of *autenticité,* on being spanking new and original. Ironically, the resulting lyrics cluster around the same themes, as narrators occupy the identical posture, gender, time frame, and attitudes as their singer-songwriting progenitors. If it's been done before, the industry thinks, it's been done to death. That kind of thinking leads to smaller, more crowded niches, until the guitars burn. But as our bass-playing physicist expounds, atoms are composed mostly of empty space. We are shot through with absence, as eternal and chimerical as Odysseus' fantasy of Ithaca. Even the *is* is not.

Not that there aren't other bands out there splicing traditions. The airwaves and iTunes stream Celtic chord progressions. The Afro-Celtic Sound System comes to mind; or the older band Horslips, which did a rock version of the *Táin Bó Cúailnge;* or Rory Gallagher, The Pogues, Fairport Convention, Flogging Molly, Gaelic Storm and their many imitators; or at the New Age end of the spectrum, Enya, Loreena McKennitt, and Clannad. Even the Chieftains have gone mainstream, recording *sessuins* with Roger Daltry, Van Morrison, and Tom Jones.

Some of these potions are powerful and they all have a kick. But at times, I wonder if the malt has been aged long enough. Even amped up, standbys like "Whiskey in the Jar" or "Courting in the Kitchen" have a hard time overcoming their hackneyed origins, notwithstanding the synthesizers and didgeridoos. At its best, the blend should develop a more complex palate, suggesting a bouquet of absence, and letting the poet— whether anonymous or merely on the road to oblivion—dissolve into myriad conditions, times, genders, species and states of life and death.

One characteristic of genuine folk music (meaning anything that's been loved so deeply by so many that the names have rubbed off) is that there's not much skin between the living and the dead. Just as Reese writes in the voice of an eighth-century crone, or a homeless drunk, or a great American Civil War poet, so the tradition glides over ephemeral distinctions: male, female; human, animal; living, dead. One verse might open, "So dig me a grave and dig it so deep," and in the next, "they dug her a grave . . . and maybe by now she's forgotten." A shipwreck lament might embark with the conventional imprecation: "All you who live at home on land, come listen unto me / While I relate of hardships great / All on the raging sea." But by the end of "The Ship Pomona," which Reese found in a ballad sheet and set to new music, we realize that we've been listening to a ghost.

I've been listening to ghosts so long I'm prone to pronounce "Ireland" "Ohio." Maybe we all slur on the late shift: Reese, Andrews, Bancroft, Homner, and Greenway—expats from homes that never were. To remind ourselves that we live in the presence of absence, we've forsworn shamrocks, shillelaghs, saints, and sheela-na-gigs, and dubbed our band after a rest area on Interstate 80 headed west from Youngstown. The place is called Brady's Leap, and if you don't believe me, the inside jacket of our first CD, *The Road To Killeshandra,* mapquests the very parish. Of course, we can't snuff out the rumors: a certain Captain Brady leapt across Ohio to escape Indians; his distant descendant once dunked a basketball against the Cork Blue Demons; a heart-sore Ithacan once biked over the wine-dark sea . . .

Perhaps we have fed the heart on fantasy, as Yeats laments. The heart's grown brutal from the fare. We know now, living in this America at this time, that brutal can mean coarse as well as violent. I don't claim that art will save us from tyranny, or that we're in danger of succumbing to a surfeit of shamrocks. But the mandate behind *autenticité* always serves a distortion that is oppression's prime requisite.

So, tomorrow night, or the night after that, we'll go back to singing Dafydd and Whitman, Browning and Cathal Bui and Sheridan and Reese. It will be a small gathering. Plenty of seats available.

As for tonight's gig: it'll be fine. We'll hang our green banner, stiffen our spines, and belt out the old tunes, as we do every year. Through the embellishments of Istvan's mandolin, or through the scent of the goatskin drum, or through the intercession of physics, tonight we will harmonize the real and make-believe. And if the green glare's too much, I'll daydream about strolling down Cayuga Street and Willow Ave, caught up in the fantasy of a return home—feeling as shot through with absence as I did as a child on 194th Street. I'll dwell on the years spent in Ireland—making friends, tending bar, studying and teaching, and yes, playing basketball. It did feel like home; but still I would find myself sometimes standing stunned at a crossroads of the here and not.

There really is "a town called Castlemaine," and "a road to sweet Athy," just as the Clancy Brothers declared. And "One evening of late" I really did "stray out of Bandon / bound for Clonakilty, making my way." Yes, it's true, "At Ballinascarthy some time I delayed," but not to "wet me ould whistle with porter," merely for a petrol stop at a plaza that might as well have been Brady's Leap. As the fuel pulsed through the nozzle, my foot came alive and my tongue found an old melody and I drifted through words and sound that came neither from airwaves, nor from the cabinet hi-fi, but from beneath, through knees and hands, into the limbic node, as my head sank to hear them better—the dead, singing of what is past, and passing, and to come.

Ginsberg in Ballydehob

THERE IS a pub in Ballydehob, West Cork, called Leviss. It's a small shoe-box of a place with a dry goods shelf, a deal table and three raw chairs, a hirsute recliner, and four stools knuckled up to the bar. Leviss is run by two spinster sisters, Nell and Julia—two beautiful old ladies straight out of "The Dead." They've owned the pub as long as any hobbit remembers.

Nell and Julia conduct business, if you call it that, the old way—shuffling in from the parlor to pull your pint, with a "Now my good man" or "Yes my girleen." But for some reason the "Celtic Tiger" seems mesmerized by this old shebeen. If you're Irish, if you've been to Ireland, if you're anyone, you've been to Leviss. Mary Robinson sat in that recliner; Van Morrison guzzled on that stool. The photo of Nell and Julia in Pittsburgh Steelers T-shirts was taken by Dan Rooney, the Steelers' owner, and last night the gent sitting next to me introduced himself as John, the chancellor of the University of Alabama. I'm told there's even a sign in an Irish expat bar on the Upper East Side pointing east: "Leviss 3000 miles."

Of course, if you're Irish, if you've been to Ireland, if you're anyone, you know this. You know (though you never heard it from Nell or Julia) Kevin Costner has had a pint here and John Hurt drops in and John Minihan drinks here (have you seen Minihan's photos of Beckett?) and John Montague regularly waters his Jamesons at Leviss.

I'd like to think that Allen Ginsberg once sat cross-legged on the saw-dust floor of Leviss. It's an old West Cork name (pronounced LEE-viss), but once a tourist is said to have asked Julia: "Leviss? That's Jewish, isn't it. Are you Jewish?" Without a blink, Julia replied, "Yes we are." I'd like to think Ginsberg heard that story. He loved Ireland—Ginsberg did—I'm told. Once, he flew to Dublin to read without fee because the director of Poetry Ireland, Theo Dorgan, offered him an Irish tweed suit. Theo says Ginsberg was buried in that suit.

The reason I want Allen Ginsberg to have been to Leviss is that I think he may be the last American poet who was anyone. I don't just mean that his name is one of the few poet's names since Whitman known to the general public; I don't mean only that he was a cultural as well as a literary figure. I mean that with Allen Ginsberg died the idea of American poetry as a story that could be kibitzed in bars like Leviss. Of course, it was Ginsberg and the Beats who challenged the story of American poetry, but that's part of the plot too: in challenging, they left it a better tale than before.

It was all explained to me at Leviss one night after closing time, blinds drawn, by a famous Irish poet. If you're anyone, you won't need to be told who.

"You had your New York poets—Ashberry and Merrill and O'Hara and that crowd," he declared, "over here"—and he slid the dregs of a Murphy's pint due east.

"And Hughes in Harlem and Williams just beyond." He thumbed two creamy circles on the bar. "And Bishop up north in the woods," he said, scaling a tricornered coaster against the base of the Smithwick's tap, "and Lowell grappling his spectral Hitler up in Cambridge.

"Then you had the Chicago gangs," he tapped a matchbox by the tureen of water, "Lee and Brooks and the other ones—Kunitz and Resnikof, the Objectivists. And above," he pointed toward the bar's laurelled mirror, "there was that mad Protestant farmer Robert Bly, and the Ohio footballer James Wright with their Deep Image.

"In the middle, the Iowa bowsers," he downed a wee jag and pucked the tumbler down, "top guns flown in from everywhere by Henry Pussycat, who plotted for decades to murther Cal.

"Down here," he snapped a pound coin on the bar, "the Southern gentry—Penn Warren, Tate, and Ransom.

"And out there," he continued, taking a gulp of Leviss's rough red vintage with his left hand and rocking the western goblet on its base, "the rebels and mumbo-jumbo mystics, Reed and Duncan, Rexroth, Snyder and Ginsberg—with one ear cocked to Nirvana and the other to Gotham."

Finally, with the topography of America completely consumed, he lurched hard left and tamped his fag in a scalloped ashtray, hard as a period.

"And there was Merwin in Hawaii—an extinct volcano."

This was the America this famous Irish poet had been reading for forty years like a palimpsest. It's the America I was taught to read also by some of the very poets nestled in the pints, ashtrays, tumblers, and wineglasses littering Leviss bar. It's a story that enriches this famous Irish poet's sense of his part in a great drama. Reading it once filled me with desire to enter its alluring web. It's a story that seems to have unraveled. He asks me, finger wagging, "Who are your contemporaries?"

If an Irish poet were asked this question, it would make for a night's great *craic.* "There's Yeats up in his eyrie and Kavanagh like Antaeus slagging him to earth and Clarke the failed priest and Devlin who almost passed for Turkish, and then the phalanx of Papists: Kinsella, Murphy, and Montague. Finally the tinder explodes and the Northern generation springs up from dragons' teeth: Longley, Mahon, and famous Seamus (like a rock star or pope, known by first name only). You've got Carson and Muldoon hooking fangs, and Simmons, grandson of the Lord Mayor of Londonderry, reincarnated in Gaeltacht Donegal. Before you could turn your head Eavan Boland swats the whole male quiff off the story, flanked by Ni Chullinean, McGuikian, and Ni Dhomhnaill—who reminds us that Irish is the only European language in which woman have always had a public voice. Then there's Cathal O'Searcaigh, who bills himself 'the Gay in Gaelic,' and the new generation of jackeens—Meehan and Boran, and the Cork boyos, Theo and McCarthy and Gerry Murphy the swimmer and Delanty over in the States with Grennan and Liddy."

If you're Irish, if you've been to Ireland, if you're anyone, you know all these characters, and you're bristling to elbow in some of the names I've missed.

Maybe there are still American poets who talk this way. Maybe, in this outpost beyond the beyonds nestled under Mount Gabriel, I'm so far from the new sources of American poetry I might as well be in Brigadoon. Maybe I just don't get it, and you're reading this with the polite boredom you feel for rustic relatives. "The barbarians are pounding the gates again, dear—this time I think they're Irish."

But I wonder, if you are my contemporary, if you read *AWP* and *Poets & Writers* (which blip their lighthouse signal promising, "there is a story; there are prizes, fellowships, and spangles galore—look at the pictures, all is well"), how would you answer the famous wagging finger? Who are your contemporaries?

It's easy to despair of making sense of the burgeoning poetry of this generation, of the three thousand books of poetry published every year, of the colonies and programs, the journals and special-interest anthologies, the workshops and conferences, each advertised with its bespangled visiting faculty—prize-adorned, internationally unknown. It's easy to feel that the story has been usurped by "Po-biz"—a cynical bestowing of destinies on well-placed cronies. It's easy to feel that coffeehouses have been replaced by computer-generated class lists. Looking at the wreckage of American poetry in the flotsam of Leviss bar, it would be easy to feel that American poetry has been debased.

Perhaps the story finally became too good, had "too many notes," and could no longer bear the weight of its own complexities. Or perhaps I'm merely being naïve. As Ginsberg's "Howl" took years to sink into American consciousness, perhaps there are readings going on right now which will seem, from the perspective of the early twenty-first century, to have been present in our minds long before most of us actually heard them. But then why is it that Irish poets seem to know the score? Why is it that when I talk to American poets we hardly even expect to share contemporaries?

If the story of American poetry has ended, then there's much to mourn. Any story which entwines poetries of different times, places, and sensibilities encourages writers to learn from one another. A. B. Yehoshua has said that if someone came to Israel and asked about writers, the same five or six people would be mentioned; but visiting Chicago he was assured of the importance of hundreds of writers. And the same name was seldom mentioned twice. Of course the result was that he learned from no one.

Donald Hall argues that contemporaries stretch ambition. The story raises the standard since every new achievement is sifted through tradition. "In my generation," Hall writes, "we wanted to unseat Homer. Now poets only want to get published in *The New Yorker*." It's worse than that now, Mr. Hall—most poets swim far below that waterline.

While tradition may torque ambition, Leviss—or the Newyorican or City Lights or Naropa or Bread Loaf—can be very small places. They can produce the kind of inbreeding that desiccated European monarchies. Reading poetry the way it's taught in university courses, with anthologies and influences and movements—all the light shining on a few blessed constellations of writers—can be a cramping affair. The belief that poetic consciousness is invested in a few people apotheosized early in life by the likes of—I won't name them, but if you're anyone you know who the king- and queen-makers are—is a life-draining belief. I'm not just talking about "multiculturalism"; I'm not trying to unseat one story by saying there are many. I'm saying that investing poetry in certain consciousnesses, however many or diverse, keeps poetry exotic and apart.

Having a story to tell both enlarges and contracts the world. By connecting us with poets from all over the world, a literary tradition expands our minds. But in the insistence that poetry resides solely in those figures, the world is shrunk to the size of a map. The story stretches us to read what we would not have otherwise understood, but it also keeps most readers alienated from their own original readings. It helps us honor those who have lived rich lives in poetry, but it can inhibit an instinct that ought to be nourished—an instinct to read originally that was very much alive in the poets named here, poets who insisted that their reading as well as their writing be untrammeled.

Don't be fooled: original readings are rare. Few people read, as Yeats says poets must write, possessing "nothing but their own blind stupefied hearts." Reading originally is a gift almost as rare as writing originally. As students we begin by reading in the context of the story, and there's no doubt this is valuable. Who today would encounter Eliot or Pound or Zukovsky or even perhaps Ginsberg outside of the American story? But reading these seminal poets doesn't affirm one's identity unless the reader develops an ability to read with fresh eyes, open to the possibility that the next poem encountered might sustain imaginative life as well as *The Divine*

Comedy. I'm not saying that there is any poetry as *good* as *The Divine Comedy.* But unless you can approach poetry with such a possibility in mind, you may be condemned never to feel the difference.

Am I suggesting a revolution? If I am, it's not to replace one set of icons for another, not to insist we install *these* poets in the canon and expel *those.* Maybe the best poems are those we have read originally.

So, my contemporaries, you ask? There was the woman in San Jose who wrote heart-wrenching lyrics, and my colleague at the University of Ibadan who opened his readings with Yoruba folk songs, and the young poet I met in Maine ten years ago and have never forgotten, and the performance poet who electrified Binghamton, and my Ohio friends—the one who's written the definitive poem on appliances and the one who's written songs James Taylor couldn't lay a finger on. There's the poet who stands before an audience and dares us to "Give me a subject" for an extemporaneous sonnet. But you've never heard of any of us. Nor do you need to, since you must have your own canon.

What will drive our ambition? What will guide our judgment? How will we avoid simply becoming self-congratulatory without achievement, handing out plaudits to smaller and blinder cliques? For one thing, I don't think we'll stop reading Dante or Ginsberg. And I hope we're not foolish enough to believe that the poets in our town or borough or neighborhood or Web site are the unrecognized descendents of the Beats or Black Mountain or Objectivists or Dada. If we are wise and humble, we will acknowledge that the story is finished. But we will recognize that in its ending, new possibilities blossom; perhaps we can read and write without allegiance to any movement—or, better, with infinite allegiances. Our ambition will be different, but perhaps as great as that of our poetic ancestors: to live, for now, without the comfort of a story, to read each poem as if this one—against all odds—could be a catalyst to change our lives, though of course knowing that we will almost always be disappointed.

"The rest I pass, one sentence I unsay."

Finally, I too long for the story. Inflecting our own voices into tunes others will hum, and humming tunes made long ago, are deeply felt needs, and I feel them as I answer the wagging finger of the famous Irish poet.

So I tell him that the best poet of my generation, the one whose work I've read with the most joy and attention, the one who has changed my life, is Robert Lunday. We met in Zaire, mapped out our ambitions together, equipped ourselves to storm Parnassus as we crisscrossed paths in New York, Cork, Provincetown, Houston, Ohio, Oregon, and Berkeley. And finally, I lost touch with him in Japan.

Robert, I've written this for you because there are so many stories in American poetry, ours is garbled, and we can't even hear each other. If you read this, old friend, write to me, c/o Leviss, Ballydehob.

My Horse's Flanks Are Spurred

I

I'M SITTING on a stool in the kitchen of Letter Cottage, five miles east of Ballydehob, West Cork, Ireland. I've come to write poetry. I have ten pages of prose from my absent host, who won't be joining me for two months. His instructions are inclusive, covering everything from which "chipper" to eat at (the one with the green awning is better than the one with the red awning) and how to use the bidet (adjust the heat so you don't scald your balls) to the dark history of Red McCarthy, the local butcher who hid his girlfriends in the meat locker. But, frankly, a thousand pages couldn't prepare me for this: I'm living in a farmhouse overlooking a valley of walled fields, ringed with western mountains and the sea.

The overwhelming strangeness of this home seems best described in prose. As Les Murray says, "Why tell this in verse? For traveling, your reasons can be the prosiest prose." Yet, despite the proliferation of prose travel writing, there is perhaps something about the experience of travel which prose cannot capture. Prose writers themselves have often struggled with the elusive nature of travel. Vita Sackville-West, for instance, says,

Travel is the most private of pleasures. There would seem to be something definitely wrong about all letters of travel, and even about books of travel. There would seem, going a step further, to be something wrong about travel itself. Of what use is it, if we may communicate our experience, neither verbally nor on paper.

Yes, travel is a private pleasure. Your voice can't be heard or your gestures understood; attempts to make sense of the strange new world resist rendering. Basho puts the quandary another way. "The trouble with poetry," he says, "is that it's either subjective or objective." Basho himself, of course, composed poetry that managed to elude that dichotomy. Ultimately, it is prose which is caught between the poles.

Living in this rustic cottage, I feel the difficulties Basho and Sackville-West express. On the one hand, New York City, my hometown, still seems like the center of the world. I feel it as I walk the streets of Ballydehob—a six-foot-three Yank in a brim hat. Dodging the tiny Aston Martins, bumping my head on lintels, reading the *Examiner* (where the lead story tells about a boy who stole a car and was confronted by a stranger saying, "Your day will come"), I feel almost Gulliverian. But when a waif yells, "Hey, Cowboy," I'm gripped by my own foolishness—not Gulliver, just Ichabod Crane. Suddenly I'm the one seen, rather than the seer; I'm as tiny as I had been huge.

How difficult it is not to reify either of these stances: the seer or seen. My first attempts to write about travel, like those of most young writers, were in prose. Returning from Africa, I was filled with the need to write about all the strange things I'd seen: the giant baobab, the python shouldered on a pole by Luba hunters, the savannah burning in the dry season, the pungent air. I wrote reams, and for years I bent friends' ears with yarns about waking up in a grass hut in North Shaba, surrounded by children who wanted to touch my white skin; or being stranded in Tanzania, negotiating with diamond smugglers for a midnight pirogue to cross Lake Tanganyika.

Although these stories seemed original, it's easy to see how they fall into genres: how they require *difference*. Stories about traveling so often seem to stylize fictive structure: the speaker is experienced, his listeners innocent; the far-off world is exotic, the reader parochial. Launching into description, the writer must hew a temporal line, as proscriptive as the hedged boreen I follow over the five Irish miles from Letter to Ballydehob: the skyview, the rolling hills, the sheep and cows are all around me, but my eyes take them in only as one part—there's a poignancy because I can never feel a part of this, except as I am apart. Yeats puts it another way: "If Shelley had nailed his Prometheus to some Welsh or Scottish rock, he would have given to English poetry the depth and breadth of ancient poetry." Yeats seems to be asking for the same nonlinear coiling that is implicit in Basho's Zen koan. Like Basho, he is pointing out a way that poetry and home can enrich and be enriched by traveling. Returning after twenty years to his boyhood home in Sligo, Yeats writes, "Although my wits have gone / On a fantastic ride, my horse's flanks are spurred / By childish memories." Memory, experience, travel and home are entwined in a poetry which might be said to be more about "voyage" than mere "travel."

The experience of traveling isn't really different in kind from the experience of being at home; it's a series of moments strung together, moments of being in and out of oneself, of feeling difference, strangeness, and feeling at home in one's body. Yet, travel writing often fences in this experience, packages it full of exotica, as if travel has nothing to do with our daily experience of being.

II

The complexity of the experience of travel is manifest to me every day I spend in Letter Cottage, because this is not the first time I have come. It's the home of the poet John Montague, and I visited Letter twenty years ago as an undergraduate and again ten years ago as an itinerate bartender and basketball player. So, entwined in the strangeness is a familiarity. Every piece of furniture radiates a flickering memory; the landscape is whorled in absences.

Of course, traveling implies return. The return gives the journey scope, and its anticipation makes the absent loom before our eyes. If prose best describes our differences, there is still a small place—a place you have to bend your head under the lintel to enter—where return is not merely implied in the narrative, but present in every second; we return and travel throughout. This doubling is strongest in poems.

In the lyric poem, some strand of shared being is celebrated or mourned, even as we realize separateness. Because poetry is not linear, and for the most part lyric poems don't linger over description, they can express something about the nature of travel that is not possible in descriptive prose. Take, for instance, John Logan's "Believe It," set in Ripley's "Believe It Or Not" Museum. The poem begins by pastiching descriptions commonly seen in such places: "There was a two-headed goat, a four winged chicken / and a sad lamb with seven legs / whose complicated little life was spent in Hopland, / California." These tongue-in-cheek lines tease with a kind of prosaic taxidermy. Abruptly, Logan dives toward the experience itself: "There is something grotesque growing in me that I cannot tell." Logan illuminates an aspect of travel that prose often misses: its quick shifts from sight to insight, even to secrecy. He concludes, "Well, I am still a traveler and I don't know where / I live. If my home is here, inside my breast, / light it up! And I will invite you in as my first guest." The poem elides point of view. The "you" of the last lines has not appeared before, and if her identity is hinted at in the dedication, "Tina Logan" is and is not the "you": she has played no narrative role as listener. Perhaps the "you" is the reader rather than the poet's daughter; either reading is possible—a subjective or objective one. Both are necessary because the grotesque is not merely reported but woven into the fabric of the lines. There is no temporal world which the poem makes cohere. Travel is a private thing, and the poem renders those aspects of it which—impossibly—escape both verbal and written accounts.

The strangeness of travel is felt differently than the experience of reading about strangeness: while a prose work usually maintains a single tone of voice, travel itself, like any other experience, is a patchwork of the familiar and the strange. Take Whitman's "Out of the Rolling Ocean, The Crowd." The poem begins with confident, dactylic rhythms and colloquial language. "Now we have looked, we have met, we have touched." Then we suddenly come upon: "Behold the great rondure, the cohesion of all, how perfect!" That strange word, "rondure," seems to crash up on the beach like a splinter from a sunken galleon. The poetry of voyage expresses what is neither subjective nor objective by opening up the spaces inside a brief lyric, so that each psychic movement seems immense. Few successful lyric poems do not occupy several worlds and experiences simultaneously, and poems of voyage often intensify these interpenetrations.

While short poems explode barriers between subjective and objective, longer poems also approach travel differently from prose. Many longer poems subvert the narrative structures they seem to employ. While these poems seem to tell a story, their interstices work against any possibility of linear coherence. Here's a section from *Captain Craig*, a long poem by E. A. Robinson:

> I cannot think of anything today
> That I would rather do than be myself,
> Primevally alive, and have the sun
> Shine into me; for on a day like this,
> When chaff-parts of a man's adversities
> Are blown by quick spring breezes out of him—
> When even a flicker of wind that wakes no more
> Than a tuft of grass, or a few long yellow leaves,
> Comes like the falling of a prophet's breath
> On altar-flames rekindled of crushed embers,—

The Captain's rhetoric sets the stage for the appearance of the shadow.

> ... But I beg
> That you forgo credentials of the past
> For these illuminations of the present,
> Or better still, to give the shadow justice,
> you let me tell you something:

As in Whitman's poem, the shifts in tone between "chaff parts of a man's adversity" and "you let me tell you something" reveal the terrain. The poem isn't merely about one man at home or far away; its intention is no less than "to give the shadow justice." The old Captain confronts memories of "men on stretchers or on beds, / Or on foul floors, things without shapes or names." He has seen so much evil that he confesses: "I have had half a mind to blow my brains out sometimes." Yet he ends his chronicle of horrors by asking, "But what has this to do / with Spring?"

What indeed? However horrible the facts, the description itself coils in nodes of being and remembrance. If the memory is exotic, the fact of remembering—its distance, its blur—is given equal primacy with the horrors recalled. However haunted April may be, the shadow can't efface Spring's joy, just as traveling can never efface the experience of being.

Perhaps the double nature of "voyage" is best revealed in poems which illuminate internal travel. The Irish *aisling*, for instance, uses the motif of travel to explore psychic terrain. Egan O'Rahilly, a late-seventeenth-century poet, wrote one of the last poems in this genre: "Gila na Gila," or in Frank O'Connor's translation, "Brightness of Brightness." The poet encounters an otherworldly queen who leads him "through reef and rock and sand / sheen and shining plain and strand" to a revelation of his personal, cultural, and political reality in the larger world:

> Brightness of Brightness lonely met me where I wandered.
>   Crystal of crystal only by her eyes were splendid.
> Sweetness of sweetness lightly in her speech she squandered.
>   Rose red and lily glow brightly in her cheeks contended.

These sound-laden lines impel us beyond mortal sight, as O'Rahilly's senses are not only engaged but nearly overthrown: "Frenzy of frenzy twas that her beauty did not numb me," he writes. Yet, however enthralling the vision, it is modulated through cunning formal rhymes, internal sound correspondences, attesting to the participation of the dead as well as the living.

The "Brightness of Brightness" is not a specter appearing to one man; she is the embodiment of a longing that binds generations. Unlike Keats's "La Belle Dame Sans Merci," whose spell leaves the speaker "palely loitering," O'Rahilly's apparition comforts the poet:

> When she heard me, she wept, but she wept for pride,
>   And tears came down in streams down cheeks so bright and comely.
> Then she sent a watchman with me to take me to the mountainside
>   Brightness of Brightness who left me walking lonely.

III

My absent host has just phoned from Albany. No, the sheep have not eaten the garden, I assure him; the byre is dry, and the water pump isn't groaning. No news on the local murder, still unsolved. He calls not merely to check in but also to connect to the home he's left. It's still winter in Albany, and here the gorse and fuchsia have begun to bloom, and the holly is putting out its small sharp leaves.

These phone conversations—the strange rip in the fabric of life—reveal another feature of modern travel. In Lubumbashi, we Peace Corps tramps would be beamed up from our hovels to the American consulate where we were treated to martinis and taped NFL games. Once I took a cassette player out beyond Kolwezi and sat on the banks of the Lualaba near the place where Stanley set out to discover the source of the Congo; there I listened to a friend's recorded voice tell of his commute from Queens to the Bronx (he even had the Throgs Neck Bridge toll collector say "hello"). The fishermen, seeing one man, hearing two voices, must have thought me one strange *msungu.*

John Montague has written two book-length poems, *The Rough Field,* and *The Dead Kingdom,* recording his personal and mythic journeys. "With all my circling, a failure to return," he writes in the last section of *The Rough Field.* But it's another of his poems, set in a train station in San Francisco and called "All Legendary Obstacles," that I'm thinking of now:

> All legendary obstacles lay between
> Us, the long imaginary plain,
> The monstrous ruck of mountains
> And, swinging across the night
> Flooding the Sacramento, San Joaquin,
> The hissing drift of winter rain.

Because I am charged with opening the poets' mail, I have come upon a recent review of his *Collected Poems* in which "All Legendary Obstacles" is critiqued. The reviewer takes issue with the line, "the long imaginary plain." The plain is real, he argues, not imaginary—it is imagined by the poet. The line should read, "The long *imagined* plain." In his desire to create a rhythmically satisfying line, says the reviewer, Montague has given in to a kind of blurriness—a failure to delineate between the state of the poet's mind and the world he encounters.

Isn't he right? The plain is imagined, not imaginary. Or is it? Here we can see Basho nodding (and shaking) his head. Because the reviewer believes the poet must choose between an objective reality and a subjective sonority, he misses the fact that poetry somehow embodies both and is wholly absorbed by neither. The power of "All Legendary Obstacles" derives in some part from the fact that the rhythm and the vision of the poem demand that the plain be, against all prose sense, "imaginary" and not merely "imagined." The poem partakes of the same tradition as the *aisling* of O'Rahilly, claiming engagement with two worlds: the imaginary and the imagined.

IV

Jamaica Kincaid has said that "a tourist is an ugly thing." A prose travel writer—even George Orwell or Jack Kerouac—is usually a privileged character, and that privilege can have especially troubling political consequences when the writer is from an imperial culture describing an oppressed one.

For instance, Henry Morton Stanley's *Through the Dark Continent*, a two-volume chronicle of his travels from the Lualaba (where I once sat listening to my friend inch through city traffic) to the mouth of the Congo River, was a best seller in the late nineteenth century, and its images of barbaric practices were for the most part accepted as prurient fact by Western readers—making the task of "civilizing" the natives much more possible and urgent. Conrad both critiques and partakes of this tradition: *Heart of Darkness* is as much about the genre of travel literature as it is about Marlow's journey. Rather than describing the forest, Conrad's Marlow resorts to phrases like "impenetrable silence." Often, Marlow's descriptive impairment is comic and deflating, a conscious ploy aimed at puncturing the high drama that characterized travel books on Africa, as when he sees "sticks" flying through the air, only to realize they are

"arrows, by Jove." Throughout, Conrad seems acutely aware of the difficul-
ties of describing what his protagonist views. However, Chinua Achebe
believes that Conrad cannot disassociate himself from the tradition of
travel literature he may have intended to critique. Achebe argues that
Conrad is responsible for Marlow, while Conrad's defenders contend that
he is making use of an accepted novelistic strategy: creating a persona
separated from the author by a patina of irony. In the context of a discus-
sion on the poetry of voyage, this disagreement takes on a slightly dif-
ferent significance. Looking at ways poets have addressed the politics of
travel, we can see that in their minds, both are true.

Unencumbered by the conventions of voice and character, a poet
can speak from a persona and at the same time take responsibility as a
lyric speaker: if there is a wall between the two, it is a porous membrane.
While prose seems to insist on individual identity, the conventions of
poetry—rhythm, pulse, and memory—disrupt the hierarchies implicit in
prose narratives, with far-reaching political effect. Had *Heart of Darkness*
been written, or more importantly, read, from this point of view, perhaps
it would have been possible to say that Conrad is and isn't Marlow.

V

There came a time when I finally became as sick of my travel yarns as my
listeners had. The stories seemed shaped by many tellings, as if they were
about someone else. To speak as "I" seemed hollow; and to usurp another
point of view seemed equally contrived, unless I somehow found a voice
that would echo my own feelings while breaking through the boundaries
of my personal experience. I needed an identity I could engage without
exploiting.

The voice I found was not that of any father or poet—or of anyone I'd
ever seen, although I'd grown up with him. It was Roger Casement, one
of the "sixteen dead men" executed after the 1916 Easter Rebellion. Case-
ment was one of many heroes of songs I hardly understood, but sang like
mantras.

At Bucknell, where I enrolled to play basketball, I was delighted to find
my childhood songs validated by Jim Carens, an English professor who
introduced me to Yeats's poem on Casement that begins, "I say that Roger

Casement / Did what he had to do." Once, to help out a friend struggling in a German class, I researched a paper about Casement's quixotic journey to Germany to recruit Irish prisoners of war to fight the British, an attempt that led to his being captured by English troops wandering "Banna Strand."

I read about the infamous "Black Diaries"—documents of homosexual love circulated secretly by the prosecution at Casement's treason trial. Falsehoods! cried the Irish—including two biographers and Yeats himself, who wrote, "They played a trick by forgery / to blacken his good name."

The Black Diaries were never released by the British, and only leaked out to the public in the 1950s. Just a few years ago, long after my own forgery of my friend's German paper, the "Black Diaries" were determined by scientific examination to be authentic.

I didn't know until after I returned from Africa and read Frederick Karl's biography of Conrad that Casement had spent most of his adult life in the Congo, where I had been stationed. As a young man, Roger Casement worked in Leopoldville, (modern day Kinshasa), helping to build King Leopold's railroads under the supervision of Henry Morton Stanley. Later he became British vice-consul to the Congo, and his exploration of the interior and his famous "Congo Report" exposed the atrocities committed by Leopold's men against the African populations. Karl believes that Casement, who met Conrad when the sailor first arrived at Matadi, was the model for Marlow.

When I saw Casement's photo in Karl's *Conrad: The Three Lives,* a gentleman reclining under a baobab tree near Leopoldville, I felt a frisson of recognition. It was Bruce Spake, a fellow Peace Corps Volunteer I'd known in Lubumbashi. The confident, distant gaze and the debonair pose (maintained even in tropic heat) had earned Spake a reputation as a ladies man, and had conferred upon Casement the sobriquet "the handsomest man in Europe." All the whorls of being and voyaging that join us. A few years ago, I met Frederick Karl in London, not as Conrad's biographer, but as "Uncle Fred," the uncle of the friend for whom I'd written a college essay on Roger Casement. Recently, Frederick Karl passed away, and Etruscan, the literary press I run, has published his last book.

Writing in the voice of Roger Casement in a book of poems called *Forged Correspondences* was not a way to novelize my travels; it was instead an exploration of the gyres that connect us. It was a way of being and traveling at the same time, by reaching toward our multitudinous connections: Montague, Stanley, Karl, Casement, Spake, Conrad, Yeats, Whitman, Logan, Basho, Kincaid, Sackville-West. We are all traveling on a road of a million crossings, modulating each other's voices.

Here is one poem from the letters of Roger Casement which I forged, partly to lend some quality of voyage to my wanderings, and partly in answer to Yeats's appeal to "Say your bit in public / That some amends be made / To this most gallant gentleman / Who is in quicklime laid."

Letter to Ireland

from: Roger Casement
to: Agnes Newman
July 12, 1903, Ibiaku

My Dear Sister,

> So your man Johnny Redmond's now the Chief.
> But Parnell lives his dream beyond his end.
> He is more real as shadowy Dead King
> than when he muddled speeches in Mayo.
> Alive, how out of place he seemed—
> that stone-face stilting clichés
> from such height he drove rain
> into the faces of his bovine worshippers.
> But I've chewed Ireland's cud long enough
> among the flies of Leopoldsville.
> And so I pocketed your letter,
> trudged east a hundred miles to answer here.
> Lost in the sun's glare, I dreamed
> I'd sip wine by a great sourceless river,
> write from some nameless well of blood.
> But here turns out to be somewhere made up—
> some place I wanted to call Eden—
> where the ice emerald that scorched my birth
> with penal laws, famine, and orange drums
> would refract into the hues of leaf and sky.

Today a man feathered like a bird
wept in my arms. He was rank
with blood and palm oil and I confess
the cold bile missionaries take
for righteousness rose in my throat.
Then I heard, between his sobs, my name—
last heard twenty years ago—*Monafuma*—
and I knew this place I wanted to be nowhere
was Ibiaku, where once a feathered chief
placed raw meat on the quivering tongue
of the young adventurer I was—
first white man he had ever seen—
saying, *take, Monafuma.* And I knew
the rumors of a massacre were true.

Nina, I don't know if you remember
spitting at the oaks where papist waifs
barbed shrikes—how we unnailed and buried
their offense to Ulster's pure air.
Today, as my chief's son scorched my mind
with images of devastation I saw
the arc of that spit flame
to a torched beehive launched by my own kin
in a barrage of fire—and it burst upon me
for the first time who I was—as if before
I hadn't known even the simplest things—
why I speak English or what love feels like.
Rory I am, here *Monafuma*—
brother to these also dispossessed.

Wiretap

I am walking backward into the future like a Greek.
—MICHAEL LONGLEY

WHEN I was growing up, the denizens of Queens walked like Dante's sodomites: heads and feet cranked arsewards. Everyone went both ways, baleful gazes aiming westward toward Manhattan, nipples stiffened toward the prefab nirvana of Long Island.

The fear and desire that unscrewed my head and cranked it around was Father. My own first, but not just him: there was Monsignor Barry, the martinet who drilled altar boys in liturgical Latin; and later, Jack Sullivan, crew-cut maniac coach of Fordham Prep, who'd skip full-jacketed into the shower for hugs. I puppied after teachers, jocks, movie stars—anything with a codpiece.

It is possible to travel a long way so contorted. Last year, my breastbone pointed toward the seacoast of West Cork, and my head screwed backward toward the cottage where the latest incarnation of my father, John Montague, ate his lunch.

In 1975, when I'd come to University College Cork as an undergraduate, it had taken three day's nerve to mount the stairs to his office. Taking a breath, I'd knocked, and hearing a muffled grunt, turned the knob and entered the musty sanctum crammed with books. Pictures hung askew—an inked Joyce, a chieftain's death mask. On the bare floorboards sat a desk spavined with tomes, and behind, silhouetted in twilight, roosted the poet, his Norman head with its crest of white hair floating above the turtleneck of a fisherman's knit sweater. His eyes were recessed deep under his brow, and tiny blue deltas marked his ruddy cheeks.

Opening a fist whose swan ring spread over two knuckles, he seated me, and after a few sweating clock-ticks I blurted that he and I came from the same neighborhood, then gushed a line of one of his poems I'd learned rocking at the cabinet hi-fi. The poet canted his aquiline nose and, side-stepping my faux pas, asked how well I knew Brooklyn, where he'd spent childhood years before returning to Ireland.

"My parents lived there," I confessed.

He swiveled toward the tiny window, and, sighing, said it was past time. I jumped to my feet, pivoted to the door, but he continued: "Past time for a pint, don't you think?"

"Yes, if you mean, I mean, that's great," I stammered.

He led me down the stairs and out into the wind of Western Road, and we matched strides past the Lee eddy with its green phone booth, past Fr. Matthew's statue and the Patrick Street Cinema featuring *Jaws,* down the alley of Oliver Plunkett Street, and into the musky warmth of the Long Valley, a tiled barroom with Tiffany lamps and trays of crustless sandwiches, radishes, celery stalks, and slabs of soda bread. Montague wended through the late-afternoon crowd and seated himself at an oval stone-heavy table, beckoning the two Murphy's pints that Humphrey, the ancient barman, had brought unbidden. With a pencil tweezed from his breast pocket, Montague nibbed dashes and question marks in the margins of the poem I'd pressed on him, all the while humming to Humphrey's flow of chatter about Hitler's private life. And so the night slid by—a blur of pints and faces—students, fans, dossers, and prognosticators dropping by to spar with the poet and check out the Yank.

"It's an arid place for the spirit, the States is," said one curly-haired youth with granny glasses and a red and white tasseled scarf, stinging me into a paean to Robert Bly, the Great Mother Goddess conference, yoga retreats, astrology, and free love.

Twitching an eyebrow, Montague said, "I wonder if Bly isn't just a mad Protestant farmer."

He knew everyone on both sides—Berryman and Lowell, Williams and Roethke, Kavanagh and Gogarty, Clarke and Beckett. He'd shared poteen with Behan and tea with Mrs. Yeats and fly-fished with Ted Hughes and crossed the Bay Bridge on the back of Gary Snyder's motorcycle—and he gossiped as if they were a pack of quarrelsome neighbors. It was the first of many magical evenings, ending with weak-kneed ambles through the sleeping city to Tivoli in mist that always seemed wetter than American rain.

Over the years, I tracked his zigzags from Albany to Cork to San Francisco to Pittsburgh, and when I'd spot him I'd elbow through the small throng of hangers-on, unfolding my newest aspirations, which he would chevron with arabesques, humming, slinging koans.

"Who are your contemporaries?" he asked once, making me think of my struggling school friends, all of them angling like me for a passport to Parnassus. And I remember the searching look he gave me when he said, "Every poet has a secret wound."

After a gala reading at the 92nd Street Y in New York, he bunked the night at 53-28 194th Street. That evening my father chauffeured us on one of his city tours, cruising through Queens, pointing out the locations of famous benders, mob deals, and shoot-outs. After one spine-tingling swerve around a traffic snarl, we ended up at Peter Luger's steak house in Brooklyn, with its charred rafters and creamed spinach and waiters looking like refugees from the Luftwaffe. My heart still pounding from the near accident, I darted glances from father to father as they traded tales of politicos, crooks, and gunmen as exotic as Gods and Fighting Men. I realized that the poet wouldn't have to ask about my wound.

That's how I came last year to be guest, cook, and driving instructor at the cottage where he spends months each year with Elizabeth, a black-haired pixie from Sarah Lawrence younger than I was. I picked my way over the sheep-dipped gorse into the kitchen, where the pair bent over the deal table, spooning bowls of my stew.

"Not bad," Montague lied.

I shrugged, tossed a wreath of keys onto the table, and said, "Let's take a spin."

We crossed the path to the antique Ibuzu I'd bought from the local garage, and I folded my legs into the right side, forgetting that everything here is backward. My pupils watched me slide into the death seat and then climbed in after. As Montague worried the stick shift, I palmed his hand, saying, "It's easy, remember? Down first, then over. And gentle with the clutch." I thought of quoting his lines, "changing gears with / the same gesture as / eased your snowbound / heart and flesh," but, remembering my gaffe on the day we first met, I bit my tongue.

"Reverse, you bastard," the poet said, and the buggy spasmed backward, scattering sheep.

Over Mount Gabriel we threaded unshouldered paths to Schull, a small crescent inlet of the sea, where we lurched to a stop and disembarked, light-headed, for an afternoon pint. Soon we were safely squatting on three-legged stools by a turf fire.

"To luck," I said, lifting my glass. "We'll need it to cross back over that mountain."

"We barely outran our shadow," Montague scoffed. "New York's where the real slaughter goes on." He turned to Elizabeth and described how my father, one finger on the wheel, had driven us through the back streets of Brooklyn, pointing out scenes of obscure calumny. The tour and our lives almost ended when my father drifted in mid-sentence through a stop sign into boulevard traffic.

"If that's how you learned to drive," Elizabeth said, "what kind of murderers will you make of us?"

The barman, a giant with a reckless beard, brought us our pints and disappeared into the lounge. Leaning in conspiratorially, Montague whispered, "This is Bailey's local, you know." I took in the small stone room, pewter mugs on the mantle, a lacquered oar and harpoon displayed on the wall. "Is that why it's empty?" I asked.

These days the mention of Ian Bailey stirred murmurs even in empty rooms. He was one of the army of "blow-ins" who swarmed into West Cork seeking a haven, wayfarers of all stripes, from Tony Blair and Jeremy Irons, whose summer homes were nestled under the shadow of Mount Gabriel, all the way down to the Austrian palm reader who ran a tea shop in Ballydehob and the paparazzi who retired from chasing Princess Di to do photo shoots of "Writers on Bicycles." The local grocery store was run by Oregon hippies; yoga seminars were advertised on pub doors.

An aspiring poet and journalist, Bailey had come from Liverpool to West Cork, took up the bodhrán, Hibernianized his name to Eoin O'Baille, hired out as gardener to the poet, and, like so many of us, slipped his verses under the poet's pencil. But all his aspirations had darkened one morning six months earlier, when the body of Sophie Toscan du Plantier, a beautiful thirty-nine-year-old French woman (and the wife of a French film producer), was discovered lying a hundred feet from her holiday home in Toormoor, near Schull. It was Bailey, working as a stringer for the Cork *Examiner,* who'd broken the story, and his intimate knowledge of the crime scene raised questions about the nature of his source. The victim's skull had been smashed with a blunt instrument—a club or hammer, he'd reported. There'd been no sign of robbery or sexual assault, and the investigating Gardai wondered if the assailant was known by the victim. Who else but a neighbor or acquaintance would be let in so late at night? Rumors swirled that an opened bottle of wine and two washed glasses had been found on the kitchen table. There were whispers that Bailey had confessed, saying, "I went too far." The only other suspect was a German businessman who committed suicide, leaving a note that vaguely implicated him in "something bad." But nothing could be proved, and though the Gardai had arrested Bailey twice, they had released him both times— much to the chagrin of the French government, which saw the botched investigation as an international affront.

Anywhere else this might have been stale news, but here, just a few miles from the spot where Michael Collins had been ambushed, politics, not sex, had always been the main motive for killing. Montague's eyes glinted with intrigue. Was it a failed love affair? Attempted rape?

"It could have been anyone," he said. "West Cork's swarming with sex mechanics."

"Listen," I said, "why don't I go see Bailey? I have my father's badge. I'll tell him I'm a New York cop brought here to consult. He wants to be a journalist. Here's his chance."

"You gobshite," Montague snorted. "Don't you know everyone already knows who you are. You can't wipe your arse around here without the world and his brother holding his nose."

And so, as the bar darkened, the talk having turned to murder, I slipped a poem out of my jacket pocket and asked the poet if he wouldn't take a look.

"It's about my father," I said. "It's a few years old. About the Crimmins case. I've been reworking it."

"The poem or the murder?" he asked, as he patted his vest for a pencil. "You haven't heard about this, I think, my dear. Tell Elizabeth about Alice."

Montague took a sturdy pull on his pint and scraped his stool to the fire as I told my fellow New Yorker about my father's case.

One August evening, midway between World War II and now, my brother and I were called in from the amniotic air of 194th Street, scrubbed down, then swatted upstairs. The vacuum roared; the liquor cabinet drawbridged to reveal emerald and gold bottles; polished ashtrays garnished the end tables. Tonight, coming for cocktails, was Alice Crimmins, whose picture was blazoned on the front page of the *Daily News,* looking like Jackie Kennedy with scarf and sunglasses.

Alice lived the life that was not admitted to exist in Queens. She had affairs and drank bourbon in lowlife bars. She divorced, remarried the same man, divorced him again. She faced straight ahead, wouldn't swerve around priest or cop. Maybe that's why she wore sunglasses at night. When her children went missing on the night of June 23, it didn't take the detectives long to point fingers. Though there were no witnesses and no physical evidence, though the first detective on the scene botched the crime-scene photos, though Alice had no conceivable motive to murder her children, the investigation torqued down on her. The evidence: the men, the booze, the sunglasses.

"If she was my wife, I'd kill her," one dick growled. But they only had to break her, and they set about grilling her at the precinct, buttonholing her boyfriends, harassing bosses at the offices where she did temp work under an assumed name. Her estranged husband they dismissed as a fool and cuckold without brains or guts enough to govern his wife, much less kill his children.

Two weeks after the disappearance, when they found the missing girl under a hedge near the old World's Fair site, they brought in Alice to identify the decaying corpse without warning her about what she was about to see. She fainted on the spot—more proof of guilt, the theatrical ploy when she'd shown no grief till then. During the months that followed, she continued to drink and dance and lure men back to her Kew Gardens apartment: a Mafioso, a Long Island real estate shark, even a cop. Guilty, guilty, guilty. But how to prove it?

So they brought in Detective Phil Brady: plaid-lapelled, purse-lipped, with a priest's bearing, peacock pheromones, and a voice that fluttered the hearts of waitresses. Though he was a CYO coach, Holy Name bigwig, and church usher, with his head cranked back to the Catholic fantasy of Queens and nose listing to port, there was, inside his florid body, an emerald that changed hue, emanating from each facet a different mood.

Because of his MP technical experience, eavesdropping from Normandy to Bohemia, he was called into the Alice Crimmins case not to investigate but to listen, assigned to wiretap Alice's apartment, her car, the booth in her local tavern. He'd sit in a dark van, listening to her lovemaking, her weeping, her cursing. This was his gift, a gift I never knew he had: to listen, to absorb the confessions of others and remain himself. Though the Alice Crimmins case spun the heads of the NYPD, there was a place inside Phil Brady that nobody was going to touch.

That August night when Alice Crimmins rang the doorbell, I sneaked out of bed and crawled to the top of the stairs to glimpse between the banister rails the famed murderess in a flame cocktail dress, highball in one hand, cigarette in the other, laughing and talking, sitting cross-legged on the couch. My father was hunched forward, my mother perched in her orange Queen Anne chair, swinging her crossed leg in time to the Clancy Brothers LP playing on the hi-fi. Suddenly, I felt the weather change. Alice shrank into herself, her beehive bobbing with cramped sobs. My mother's leg froze; my father rose from his recliner and glided like a bearish cloud to the couch. Whispering, he draped his huge arm over her shoulder. I'd never seen him hold my mother the way he held Alice that night, and she sobbing and sobbing.

What I didn't learn until years later, when I read *The Alice Crimmins Case,* is that our basement had been as carefully prepared for Alice's visit as the rest of the house. There, amid the flotsam of unmatched socks and old trophies, three detectives hunkered over a massive tape recorder. What could they have made of what they heard? A scratchy voice whispering, "There, there"? A woman's sobs? Maybe the hidden mikes were sensitive enough to catch the pounding of a child's heart.

Telling the story in a quiet pub in the penumbra of another murder, I conjured up Alice Crimmins, mounting the stairs quietly to my childhood.

"How did it end?" Elizabeth asked.

"She was convicted, finally, after two trials. Served eight years. I heard that she moved to Florida when she got out. She'd be in her eighties now, if she's alive."

"Did you write this before your father died?" Montague asked, having turned back to us now, his glass empty.

"Yes."

"Did you show him?"

"All he said was, 'you got some facts wrong.' Nothing about the poem—about him and me and how I couldn't ever say what I needed to."

"Maybe he was afraid," the poet said.

"It was me who was afraid." I said. "Not to die—I didn't even squeak in the backseat when he nearly killed us, remember? I was afraid to face. . . ."

"Face what?"

I had no answer. The barman had slipped back in, and watching him glance at us sidelong, I thought of Ian Bailey, who'd once frequented this bar, having come to Ireland yearning for a home he'd never known. Was it his specter that paralyzed me? His words, stammered, revised, submitted to a poet, swallowed, finally congealed into a hammer propelled by madness. I knew his failure. Was I terrified of walking mute and outlawed in his shoes?

My father taught me everything except this: to keep a place inside that stays untouched. And my father, in the guise of an Irish poet, slid my poem, marked with his cuneiform, across the table, saying, "You might make something of this."

Meaning not, as Phil Brady would have meant, a life. Meaning, I hope, a filament entwining words and world.

"Enough blather. Let's hear the poem," the poet said.

Wiretap

How could Detective Brady and his perky wife
storm upstairs to enforce lights out
when the bleached blonde cross-legged on their sofa
had strangled her two children?
                    Perfectly safe,
I moled between the two top banister rails,

Eavesdropped a spill, a laugh, and something clicking.
She must have sloshed her cocktail,
slipped her heels off. Soon,
muffled sobs, my father's soothing tenor, *there there*.
Unthinkable now to slink back to my room,
dream murder mounting the stairs barefoot.
Maybe the girl puked up the night of June 23rd
or the boy sassed—maybe it was finally
too much—the waitressing, the boyfriends,
divorce in Queens in 1965.
Unthinkable—solitude a thing I couldn't bear—
still is—internal voices whisper *home*
and twice they've nearly had me married.
The cops had Alice's Ford or something close
reliably witnessed cruising 3:30 AM.
Next day, they chalked one tiny corpse near Kew Gardens.
The other—the girl—nested in the weeds
of the World's Fair for two weeks.
Once a year, when my father picks me up at Kennedy,
we pass the silver skeleton Fair globe
without a word for that grim search,
the Crimmins trial—the sentence long since passed.
Although his Queens is a kind of wax museum
(at this gin mill Fuentes outbled Diaz,
at this ristorante Anthony Grace fell)
his famous case—the one they made a book—
this one he hates, because, he says,
my mother is not "perky" and some facts are fudged.
True, as the book says, mick bloodhounds
were bent on nailing that bitch Crimmins—
their eyes glazed over when she claimed
she checked the sleeping kids at 3 o'clock.
Instead, they teased clues from her beehive hairdo,
they sleuthed right through the shades
she donned for Daily News splash pics.

Kelly was stone stubborn, Pierig horny
to make second grade. They had the car,
they had the coroner pinning the first death
near 2 A.M. Still, they needed a mole—
someone they trusted, someone she would trust.

In *The Alice Crimmins Case*,
Detective Brady's manner is "confessional"—
and after twenty years, a heart attack,
cancer and four strokes, still is.
Clasping his hands, he hoods the dinner table
and the fact I am a liberal atheist
exudes from me like sweat
but never does the conversation stray
as far as who he is.
                    Mention the Crimmins case
and something inside him clicks,
something is welled in echoes,
something behind his eyes begins to spin
like the reel-to-reel that hunkered on his desk,
state-of-the-art, 1965. I was
too busy jerking off and freebasing
pure heresy at Fordham Prep
to eavesdrop cop tapes, but last month,
years after I stormed out the 53-28
screen door swearing new life, I spied,
wedged on a lost shelf in the basement
of a Berkeley used book shop, the familiar
discounted title. Sobs welled up
in that California cellar, most distant point
in the farthest orbit around Queens I'd dared,
so far I feared that if I took two steps,
nothing would pull back.
Yet, thumbing that pulp, I realized
my father had traveled farther.

What did it mean in 1965
to tape those sobs, then turn his back
on Kelly and Pierig, press *erase*?
Queens was a world honeycombed with generations,
a safe place for white men and most women.
What did it take to replay for the defense
proof the coroner fudged time of death?
The hack who wrote *The Alice Crimmins Case*
and juiced those sobs to hawk his schlock exposé
invents "two sleepless nights" for Detective Brady
before he wakes Alice's sad-sack lawyer.
But when I think of that ineffectual,
or just imaginary phone call
I see a door open and my father
take two steps into nothing—
but for all my traveling, I'll never know—
and though I want him not to go on
being him, me being me,
I haven't stopped, nor found a way
to tell all this to anyone I love.

PART THREE

The Poetry Broadcasting System

The Poetry Broadcasting System

THE WEIRDNESS starts at the Port Authority where I step up to the cage and gulp, "Where do I get the bus for the Poetry Festival?" The clerk points across the lobby; the machine spits out a ticket. No stares, no sniggering; the Port Authority Veil remains unrent. The weirdness deepens when I disembark into a beautiful autumn day in Waterloo, New Jersey. I know this place, though I've never been here before. I've seen it on a Bill Moyers Special, *The Power of the Word,* in which Bill, in his down-home dulcet, explained that poetry wasn't as forbidding as we had thought. He planted his elbows on one of the fencerails right over there, against this same backdrop of pond and stone bridge, and said that there'd been a mistake: poetry wasn't elitist or elusive; it was about folks just like us in the PBS audience. The camera panned to a throng of khaki, then zoomed on a series of rapt faces.

The people milling about today look just like the people who milled for Bill. High school students gaggle around teachers in parkas; graybeards in lumberjack shirts study festival programs. Celebrities mingle with the crowd: Billy Collins sips from a plastic cup; Lucille Clifton mounts a golf cart to be ferried to the next event; Jorie Graham signs a book. There are circus-style tents and carnival vendors. There's a gift shop and a makeshift Borders. It's a day at a county fair.

I follow the program map to the Farmstead Tent where Tony Hoagland tells us to write about things that poems have never before touched: for instance, the way a plastic grocery bag bulges just before breaking. In the Braw Pond Tent, Mark Doty says we all carry "god consciousness"; while in the Church, Gerald Stern spins a yarn about teaching seventh-graders in Pittsburgh. It's almost lunch time. As I wrestle a gyro, an amplified screech pierces the autumn air. "I want to straangle Rumsfeld . . . I want to straaangle Rumsfeld . . . I want to straaaangle Rumsfeld."

By the time I reach the Main Stage Tent, curds are dripping down my jacket. A tiny figure, blurred silver in my misted specs, shakes invisible tambourines over her head. "I want to straaaangle Rumsfeld." Her voice scrapes over the thrilled crowd, climbing a raw scale. Who is that, I wonder. I scan the list. Why, it's Anne Waldman. Overhead, the camera grip cranes over the amphitheatre, the crowd still abuzz. It's delicious: where else could such a scream be so welcomed? Despite the red-blue quilt of the country, it turns out that every attendee at the Geraldine Dodge Poetry Festival wants to kill the Secretary of Defense.

Personally, I've never met the guy. But I've seen his college photo in a Princeton bar. It was a Dorian Gray moment. He looked eerily like his future self, as if the smugness and venality just needed a half century to worm their way to the surface. Yet, he was twenty: just a frat boy in a V-neck sweater. Were that kid to show up here today, I do not believe that any of these thousand poetry enthusiasts would offer violence. Still, we bond in our desire to strangle Rumsfeld.

Why not? It's exhilarating to join in the surge of a pure emotion. It makes me feel Bill's "power of the word" to unite and inspire. Waldman is the last reader and the crowd pours out of the tent to buy lunch, surf Borders or claim front-row seats for the next panels. I feel good. I've seen a lot in a few hours. I cross over the covered bridge, lean on the rail fence, and gaze across the shimmering pond, just as Bill did. A white spire rises above the tawny forest leaves.

During the afternoon rounds, two panelists in separate tents joke about strangling Rumsfeld. Already Waldman's performance has been woven into the festival mythos, a moment that will be talked about in prep schools and Upper East Side apartments long after Andrew Motion's meditations and Linda Hogan's sketches of the Native American West and

Linda Gregg's koans are forgotten. Tramping out to the parking lot, I try
to figure out why this should bother me. Thousands of people descend
on New Jersey to see a score of poets from five continents read in a wide
variety of modes. If some readings yield more immediate pleasure than
others, so what? Everyone was heard; everyone was applauded. As for the
Rumsfeld bit: I love impassioned speech. Waldman's hyperbole galva-
nized a moment. And cursing is a prime mandate of poetry. From Milosz
through Baudelaire, from Tu Fu to Horace, poets have forged out of help-
less anger a language of power and vision. So what's missing here?

I've seen some great sorcerers in my day. I remember Amiri Baraka in
City Lights chanting "Anti Reagan Anti Reagan Anti Reagan Anti Reagan"
until meaning was flensed from the bare syllables. I remember walking
the streets of Derry one troubled twelfth of July, feeling mummified in
Union Jacks, and slipping into a pub to hear "Only Our Rivers Run Free."
I remember Albany in 1991, when William Heyen delivered a poem on the
Gulf War that ended with the unforgettable line: "And I knew then what
had become of the American whose heart had been cut out." I remember
an anti-Mobutu rally in Lubumbashi which was kicked off with a Luba war
chant. I love poetry sung and said in public—the vigor of imprecation, "the
power of the word."

In its poetic form, the curse is never just a scream; it doesn't merely
express disgruntlement. The poetic curse juxtaposes human frailty against
the force the poet conjures. It's a dizzying distortion of scale that sets a
tiny presence against a vast absence. In raw form, curses involve powers
beyond the poet's ken, as they call on the eternal to influence—or at least
witness—a temporal event. "It so happens," begins Neruda in "Walking
Around," "I am tired of being a man." In his manic chronicle, he cites "tai-
lor shops and movies . . . a river of beginnings and ashes . . . The smell of
barber shops . . . elevators . . . roots and tombs": the whole rag and bone
shop of the everyday, all of which makes him "weep aloud." In its encyclo-
pedic breathlessness, the curse releases a kind of blessing, which finally
drips down laundry in "slow filthy tears." Presence tints absence, just as
rhythms color the world they call into being.

Sometimes curses swirl power into meaning by tumbling down a lin-
guistic flight of stairs. Addressing the thief of his prize duck, the epony-
mous Nell Flaherty of an old folk song wails a quirky, rhyme-driven rollick:

"May his spade never dig, May his sow never pig / May each hair on his wig be well thrashed with a flail. / May his door never hatch, may his roof have no thatch / May his turkeys not hatch, may the rats eat his mail." The same technique darkens "Daddy," where Plath descends in only a few stanzas from "I used to pray to recover you / Ach, du" to "Chuffing me off like a Jew. / A Jew to Dachau, Auschwitz, Belsen."

Absence can enter by allusion, as in Frank Bidart's "Curse," which prays, in regard to the 9/11 terrorists, "May what you have made descend upon you." In his Notes, Bidart makes explicit his debt to Dante, explaining that his poem is based on a notion put forward in *The Inferno* (perhaps the greatest of all curses) that "what is suffered for an act should correspond to the nature of the act." Or the aura of absence can be invoked by indirection, as in Thomas Lynch's "To the Ex-Wife on her Birthday," which proposes a chronicle of ills, including "green discharges, lumps, growths . . . dry heaves, hiccups, heartbreaks, fallen ovaries"—all of which the speaker "does not pray" befalls his ex-wife. Always, a good curse demands tension between the ephemera of the poem and the ineluctable powers conjured.

Waldman too displays craft; her technique manifests itself in her performance. She does not merely scream, "I want to strangle Rumsfeld"; she sings it, plays it on her fingers. The production of such volume from such a tiny figure represents a technical feature of the poem, highlighting the contrast between the great and tiny. Instead of rhyme or meter or refrain or rhetorical balance, she torques things up by juxtaposing her small body against the image of arms powerful enough to reach across the malls and pastures of New Jersey, down 95 South and into the Pentagon situation room to throttle the Secretary in his swivel chair. Were the poem performed by someone of greater corpulence, the threat might have contained more menace, but less poetic power.

Yet here at the Geraldine Dodge Poetry Festival, that trope fails. I don't feel those slender arms reaching perilously across turnpikes; whatever power Waldman's curse generates is muffled by the tent and absorbed by the trees and fields of Waterloo, New Jersey. While Donald Rumsfeld remains a global threat, I do not feel his shadow disturbing the day's tranquility. That's what I miss: the Other, the necessary shadow—what Billy Collins in another tent calls the "duality of poetry." Such duality need not be comprised in the text; it can also be generated by the friction between a poem and its presentation. But without it, whatever power that a poem can muster wanes.

While the gatherings in San Francisco, Derry, Lubumbashi, and Albany were equally partisan, membership in those audiences seemed to heighten individuality. My identity as a liberal, or an Irish Catholic, or a Peace Corps Volunteer, or an American, felt poignant when I heard it voiced with such mesmerizing fragility. The presence of the Other was tangible in the air, darkening and energizing the connection between poet, audience, and curse.

In his play, *The Death of Cuchulain,* Yeats explores the central role of the Other in nurturing identity. The play opens with an old man in motley complaining that if there are more than fifty or a hundred in the audience, he won't be able to protect himself from those people educated by the book societies. Clearly, Yeats needed to count his listeners one by one. What would the old Sligo iconoclast have thought of PBS?

Yeats's tirade may not have been about thinning out the house, but about reaching the individual psyche. What if within each of us there's a private person—say, an innocent-looking kid in a V-neck. How can that kid's face ever be revealed, except when confronted with the Other—the countenance warped by decades of corruption?

Impassioned speech that seeks the condition of poetry demands an unmediated confrontation: the necessary sense that we are few and precious and otherwise voiceless. At the Geraldine Dodge Poetry Festival, I do not feel like a member of a community—call it "the people"—whose identity is forged or expressed by the poet's voice. Instead, I feel like a member of "the public"—that shuffling mass we point at but to which we never truly belong. The public wants this, we say. The public leans toward that. We talk about the public as if it's our simple cousin—the one you have to address a little slowly and loudly. At the Geraldine Dodge festival, I feel dipped to the gills in the public.

This is the source of the sickly feeling: in the groomed backdrop of tents and pond and bookstore and bus-filled parking lots, no shadow can lurk. I can't feel the chill of Rumsfeld's eerie penumbra; the warping of his photograph from collegian to Rasputin does not tint Waldman's poem, which is reduced to a performance. For this I don't blame Anne

Waldman, whose career as a gadfly has spanned thirty years. I don't blame Bill Moyers, personally. He seems like a nice guy, interested in the arts. I blame the "media-tion" that he represents. It's here, even though he isn't. It's in the tote bags and the souvenir bookmarks. It's in the PDF programs and the hooked-up speakers and the video cameras sweeping manicured lawns; it's in the orange security vests and the A–M/N–Z ticket lines. It's in the autumn air that seems to affirm that poetry is healthy and accessible and that anyone can have some and it won't hurt too much either.

Do I need poetry to be clandestine, delicate, arcane, or elitist? I don't think so. Do I want poetry to abandon its traditional place in the political sphere? No, no, no. Let Frost anoint Kennedy and Sandino harangue Nicaragua and Country Joe rock Woodstock and Churchill recite Tennyson and Pearse summon Cuchulain to his side. But let there be no moderation and no moderator. Let the curse come directly from the people's embodiment—even if she has no podium or microphone. Let the invective spray from one spit-flecked mouth outward through a wildish gathering to sizzle on the anvil of the unchangeable and indifferent world.

While I admit that even after his resignation I might wish Rumsfeld breathless, and I confess too that I'm secretly thrilled by the busses and tents and logos, the way I cheer the underdog in a championship match, I worry that the spectacle, attended by the camera-endorsed public, might blur the hues in poetry's spectrum—from political outrage to private meditation. When I think of the other poets who read in the big tent, I wonder if perhaps our internal volume wasn't ratcheted up too high to hear their most delicate nuances. Worse, is it possible that poets themselves—who are, after all, human—might be tempted to write more accessible poems just to compete? Surely poets of such eminence are immune from skewing their work toward the public, but apprentice poets in the crowd that day could be excused if they were tempted toward performances that spiked the applause meter.

Yes, Bill has much to account for. Whenever the word "poetry" is used to describe speech or song that depends on public consumption instead of formal dynamism and complexity, we shrink the space—already very small—for such speech to move us. And move us it does. While the public views *The Power of the Word*, the people continue to read Yeats, each one one at a time.

Back in the city, I'm released into the flow of traffic. In the subways I feel the thrum of the rails under my soles as I sway shoulder to shoulder with my fellow faceless straphangers. How intimate and inaccessible we are. It's a paradox only a poem could describe. "When I am alone / how close my friends are," says Antonio Machado; "when I am with them / how distant they are."

Poetry can reach multitudes, but it can't brook a crowd.

The Shapes a Bright
Container Can Contain

A BOOK. The idea of a book of poems. The gloss. The slender spine. A collaboration among poet, artist, designer, editor, reader. Echoing hinted plots, untried paths; yet also delicate, brief: the pleasure of an afternoon. It can seem an icon from a yet uncanonized hand, bringing news that stays. My first was John Montague's *The Rough Field,* which I came upon in Cork a few years after its 1972 release from Dolmen. How it felt to hold that eighty-four page volume of Times Roman stanzas with their ominous gaps and Delphic montage interspersed with quotes from bedfellows as strange as Che Guevera and the Great O'Neill. The solo journey; the cultural undertaking. The noble frontispiece, designed by Liam Miller, adapted from an Elizabethan woodcut of cottages put to the torch, called "The Image of Irelande with A Discoverie of Woodkearn," and subtitled, "Ulster 1961– 1971." The stylized horror, stamped with the shield of the United Irishmen of 1798 and framed by calligraphy: "old moulds are broken in the north / in the dark streets firing starts . . ." The humble grandeur of the opening lines: "Lost in our separate work / We meet at dusk in a narrow lane." No book but one from that time so resonates, even now, with the pangs of Ulster congealed in a red ink-splash of ancient blood seeping all the way to Berkeley and beyond: "streets of Berlin / Paris, Chicago / seismic waves

/ zigzagging through / a faulty world." My second edition paperback, unearthed in a quayside bookshop, is rusted with rings of Guinness.

Then there was Kinnell's *The Book of Nightmares,* a sequence of ten poems in the voice of a man—"concert of one / divided among himself"— chanting into the dark. So many more: Sharon Olds's *Satan Says,* a first book that seemed to emerge from two lifetimes; and Pinsky's *An Explanation of America,* with its Horatian Epistles and porno film critiques, elucidating the world to a young daughter, reminding me now of another daughter conjured in Snodgrass's peerless *Heart's Needle.*

These were not opuses like *The Cantos, The Maximus Poems, A,* or *Paterson;* they lacked the heft of tomes thick enough to stop bullets. The great modernists didn't crave mere books; they patterned their masterpieces on sacred texts, hermetic, encoded—"poems including history." Neither did the Romantics yearn for the kind of books I'm talking about here. Their longer poems were mythic or pastoral, meditative or Byronic. And of course before that there were the spicy essays of Pope and Dryden, manic with reason, and the epic's doleful drumbeat, marshalling poems, which, as Johnson said of *Paradise Lost,* no one could wish longer.

I won't even get into anthologies. There's something unwholesome about holding a sheaf on your lap, shifting postures, your thighs going numb, your wrists arthritic. It's overwhelming, all those "great" poems crowding forward like wraiths demanding blood. And the journals tint me envious or enraged.

A "Collected"? Too definitive. And more than likely it will offer, instead of apotheosis, the wayward wreckage of a life plan.

"Selecteds"? Too much like Greatest Hits. In a time when poems conceive their own form—whether New Wave or Deep Image or New-Expansive or Language or Post-Cereal-Structuralist-Krispies—an anthology or periodical or even a Collected or Selected can swim before your eyes like a Petri dish.

What I want this warm Ohio September Sunday afternoon is a book. A chance to spend some time—but not too much—with a single presence. Such a work, printed while the composition is still warm, reflects one blossoming consciousness, playful but fully intended. Like a good performance, a book allows a poem to breathe—and surely, amid today's jangle of slogans, Muzak, and blather, a poem needs a bright, sturdy container.

Not a textbook (who can even read the Nortons crabbed with numerals?). Not a Web site with amebic pop-ups. Not a bus or a radio show. Call me a Luddite, but I want a book.

But how to make one? Can't be too hard. After all, every season sprouts new bushels. Win a contest. Ply a friend. Learn PageMaker. Spam the market. Buy a stapler. Then stuff verses till they squint. Since most lyric poems aren't composed with a finished book in mind, it may come to that. But when it does, you may find you don't have a book; all you've got is a clot. So you rearrange, fiddle, spread them out over the kitchen floor. You shuffle, dog-ear, append. You phone your pals. If this is your first "kitchen cabinet," your job's even harder, since the poems buttering the tile are the ones that taught you how to write. You love them all, though they get along no better than princely siblings. More elbowing. A purge or two. A few floaters clog the drain. And still no book.

Some say, fashion a book on the same principles which animate its poems; each poem introducing, developing, or recapitulating a theme whose thread runs through the entire work. Fair enough. This certainly makes sense in books which play with or against a traditional form. Scanning a new crown of sonnets, we glimpse the glitter of crowns from Heaney to Sidney, refracting new surfaces into multidimensional shapes. Suspense torques the tension: how can these sonnets stay fresh? What new twist? What ploy? Cole unscrews rhyme and meter; Carruth ratchets them up; Hacker turns the gender table; Berryman abracadabras table, house, and air. My newest fave is H. L. Hix's sequence, "The God of Windowscreens and Honeysuckle," which raises the crown-tines to a new high: fifty-six. Four seasonal sonnets lend their lines as building blocks to a sonnet for each week. Winter's second line provides the second line for Winter's first week, etc. Such delight in pushing the inside of the envelope.

But what about those poems whose form isn't signposted by shadows? The formative principles of some poems seem so deeply embedded in an original moment that to stretch them over the length of a book would be like racking taffy. How to organize such poems so that each retains its sheath of silence while cohering as a greater whole? It's tempting to group by theme or setting. All poems on the subject of Spring step over here, please. All New Jersey poems over there. Yet, theme alone isn't enough to make a book. Without the tension of a sequence like "the God of Windowscreens and Honeysuckle," how will all these Jersey Springer poems avoid degenerating into a mob?

How to make a book instead of a collection? If your poems are elusive, amorphous, and translucent, you might try setting them in a structure that casts its own network of shadows. Inhabit this place. Work its depths. Play on its high wires. Just as the Romantics housed poems in myth, the neoclassicists in essay, and the Elizabethans in epic, our books of poems breathe in the atmosphere of the dominant literary form of the day. And for us, friends, on this side of the millennium, that bright shiny container is the novel.

Think about it. Novels saturate us. They're in movies, on TV, in supermarkets; they claim prime acreage in bookstores; there's a paperback facedown on your bathroom floor, another on your night table. When someone says, "I'm reading a great book," what do you think of? Fact is, whether we wish it or not, our readers are pickled in novels. If you've taught freshmen, you know that their first task is to read a poem as a poem, not as a story: "Slow down," we tell them. "Hear the music." Immersed in novels, we find it difficult to attend to the nuance, dissonance, misdirection, and systematic derangement that characterize poems. Everything is read through fiction's prism.

Not that books of poems should mimic novels, or be held hostage to their conventions. The goal (unless you're Vikram Seth!) isn't to write a novel in poems, but to suggest the feel and breadth of a novel, and in so doing, allow each poem to be read in its own eternal time and infinite space.

How can books of poems have the breadth and feel of a novel without billowing into narrative?

First, impetus. Novels hurtle into an imagined universe, impelled by generative lines which seem encoded with the DNA of the entire work. "Call me Ishmael. . . ." "Stately, plump, Buck Mulligan. . . ." "Many years later, as he faced the firing squad, Colonel Aureliano was to remember that distant afternoon when his father took him to discover ice. . . ." Borne by self-created logic, their primary sentences feel discovered rather than invented. And in this regard, the opening stanzas of books of poems can reveal even more than novels' first lines, since rhythm, line length, texture, and style are highlighted. It can set the theme, as in the unmetered, straightforward opening to Carolyn Forche's *The Country Between Us:* "We have come far south." It can set the emotional tone, as in the last lines of Milton Kessler's first poem in *The Grand Concourse:* "My new job's / to wave them in. / Hello freighter, / hello tanker / Welcome, welcome / to New York." It can introduce voice and conflict, as in Jim Daniels's *Punching Out:* "*This is your first day?*" Bush asks. / *I been here 22 fuckin' years.*" It can play the first minor-key notes of a symphony, as in Brigit Pegeen Kelly's eponymous *Song:* "Listen, there was a goat's head hanging by ropes from a tree." Or it can lay the blueprint for an architecture, as in "Heroic Simile," from Robert Hass's famous *Praise:* "When the swordsman fell in Kurosawa's *Seven Samurai* / in the gray rain, / in Cinemascope and the Tokugawa dynasty . . ." More than novels, books of poems depend on orchestrated powers which reveal themselves in the first stroke. First lines in first poems are more than first lines of a poem: they are first lines of a book.

Then there's scale. James called novels "baggy monsters," but in fact their girth produces a complex relationship with time. Whether or not a novel is cinched tight, the very experience of reading imposes structure: time in the novel contrasts with the temporal act of scanning pages. Novels distort Aristotelian unities, dwelling for hours in a fictive moment or sweeping through a century in minutes. The overall effect is to present an imaginatively coherent world, suspending or at least counterpointing the reader's quotidian world. When the book drops open on the belly and the hat brim droops, somehow the novel's world continues to turn.

The best books of poems share this quality. While they don't map a fictive cosmos, they do thread gracefully, relentlessly, through a temporal schemata that may be wildly distorted, but never abandoned. Perhaps the postmodern novel's experimentation with time and scale has prepared readers for poetry's more radical dislocations. But I would argue another cause. Modern poems seldom present the novel's smooth texture, the uninterrupted dream in which the border between the reader and the text dissolves. Instead, textured sound, linguistic density, inventive typography, and alogical progression intensify readers' sense of the poems as artifice or organism, while at the same time heightening awareness of themselves as beings moving through time: eyes gleaning the page, voices testing syllables. It's hard to completely forget your body. Poems, like rhythmic mantras, leave us paradoxically *here* and *elsewhere.* Reading too many at a sitting leaves me dazed. When this experience of natural artifice is feathered with a patina of theme, or texture, or thrum of a single voice, it can impart the impression of having read much more than is actually there—the way Irish rain just feels wetter. Reading a good book of poems is like traveling unknown terrain at night, glimpsing in each lightning bolt a swatch of vastness.

Another way to project scale is through refraction. Earlier I mentioned that besides *The Rough Field,* at least one other great book of poems came out of The Troubles in Northern Ireland. I was thinking of Seamus Heaney's *Field Work,* which appeared in 1979. While many of the poems in *Field Work* address the conflict directly, it is the last poem, a translation from the thirty-third and thirty-fourth cantos of *The Inferno,* which expands into novelistic breadth. In "Ugolino," Heaney recounts the fratricidal strife that leaves Florence's traitorous Count "gnawing at [Archbishop Roger's] neck and head." It's a compelling scene of betrayal, imprisonment and starvation leading to hell's frozen cornice, and yet, for all of Dante's bitterness, the poem's placement on the last pages of a book by an Ulsterman writing in the midst of his own hell infuses new meaning into both *The Inferno* and *Field Work.* When Heaney translates, "Pisa, your name is like a hiss / slithering in our country's grassy language," I hear an echo of *Paisley.* When he explodes, "may a huge dike / of islands bar the Arno's mouth. / Let Capria and Gorgona dam and deluge / you and your populations," he gives voice not only to Dante, but also to his own heart and people. His refracted curse is more powerful than any that could be leveled eye-to-eye; more importantly, it opens and bridges, in these few pages, a chasm of five hundred years. How long would a novel take to stretch its legs that far?

The last step is to make a beautiful object. Perhaps because novels are produced by big cost-conscious publishing houses, or perhaps because they feel steam-sealed in words, resistant to other means of apprehension (don't we distrust the adaptation's celluloid bloat?), works of fiction seldom feature memorable covers. But when I think of books of poems that I love, I often think of the cover: the cloud-wreathed Tower of Babel in William Greenway's *Ascending Order;* the don't-try-this-at-home exploding shoes of Nin Andrews's *The Book of Orgasms;* the livid cave painting of Robert Lunday's *Mad Flights.*

While page counts don't reach triple figures, books of poems can still seem voluminous, in part because cover art opens another dimension— "mirror on mirror mirrored . . ." Unlike novels, poems deploy a variety of modes that permeate the barrier between the reader and the uninterrupted dream, making it possible to integrate visual art into the kaleidoscope of sensation a book of poems engenders. Cover art can do more than represent a book's contents. It can enter into a dialogue, as in William Heyen's *Confessions of Doc Williams,* where George Bellow's pastoral seascape not only references one poem but also fingers the grain of trim lines running throughout the work. By embracing vision—as well as silence, music, and speech—slender books of poems can feel as rampant as any novel.

Running Etruscan Press, I've had the pleasure of being involved in the making of books of poems, seeing them go from manuscript to the cartons trucked in from Thomson-Shore. I love tearing through the Styrofoam, taking in that new-book aroma. Holding a fresh copy linted with peanuts, opening the skin-smooth paper to see these familiar poems set in their elegant new typography—it's always a shock even after the proofs and galleys. It wasn't until I touched the gunmetal jacket of Heyen's *Shoah Train,* featuring *Trains* by Samuel Bak with its eerie smokestacks jutting from bestial machinery, that I felt the full impact of those magnificent poems. H. L. Hix's *Shadows of Houses* features Sarah McKenzie's photograph-miming oil painting, *Aerial #52,* in a wraparound design. The warped perspective almost prepares the reader for the sinister permutations of Hix's genius. Bruce Bond's *Cinder* first came to Etruscan under another title. Bruce mulled several possibilities, each casting a slightly different light on the book's nuanced, complex poems. When he came upon *Cinder,* he also found the painting which would adorn its cover: *The Isle of the Dead,* by nineteenth-century artist Arnold Boecklin. Title, image, and poems formed a new book, nascent but unseen until they coalesced into their final form.

Speaking of *Cinder,* other great titles come to mind: Charles Simic's *Return to a Room Lit by a Glass of Milk,* Amiri Baraka's *Preface to a Twenty Volume Suicide Note,* Bill Knott's *Autonecrophilia,* Tony Hoagland's *What Narcissism Means to Me.* So much better than *"Something and Other Poems."* Come to think of it, why must a book be titled after one of its poems at all? Of the books I've mentioned here, *The Country Between Us, The Rough Field, Punching Out, Cinder,* and *Shadows of Houses* all found their titles in the interstices between the poems, as did two of my books: *Weal* and *Forged Correspondences.* In my case, I didn't find the titles alone. Somebody found them with me.

Assembling my own "kitchen cabinet," I was lucky enough to have a novelist and a painter on call. It sounds like the setup for a joke, but it led to some of the most serious work I've ever participated in. While I sorted poems by zip code (Ireland, Africa, Queens, California), my novelist was knocking around in the crawlspace, soldering pipes and valves. Thumbing through that book from ten years ago, I still enjoy opening to a random page to see how Bob Mooney found the thread between poems that had been conceived in different times and moods. Another thing he taught, yelling up from that psychic underground: cut till you bleed. Some mid-nights I still find myself apologizing to ghosts turned away from the table of contents. But listening to Bob's voice, I learned not only about putting a book together, but about making the next one. Now, however intense my attention on the moment, some place under the floorboards vibrates. I can't put it into words. But I don't have to, because there was someone else in that kitchen, working on the roof. His name is Bob Carioscia, and images of his paintings have appeared on three of my books—as well as on the one you're holding in your hand. At one time or another during the making of a book, I take a trip to his studio in Little Italy, where I find a magical store of dream visions to array old poems and generate new ones. One hangs above my desk. It portrays a house outlined with real twigs and embedded in a fiery sky above a fish-infested sea. Inside the twig house is a painted one, and inside that, a man holds a picture of a man. Is it a book? A secret? A soul? In the flaming sky appear the electrified words: NOT KNOWING, RELYING ON INTUITION. Good words to make books by.

On Becoming a Poetry Editor

IT'S SATURDAY night. The living room is strewn with paper. The Indians are on with the volume down. I slit open the next envelope, take another sip of lukewarm coffee. I am a poetry editor.

How does one become a poetry editor? Yeats seemed to think it a by-product of hair loss (bald heads . . . edit and annotate the lines . . .). In my case, the senior editor was up to his eyeballs and asked me to help out. "Why not?" says I. Dan Bourne is a fine poet; he plays guitar and shoots hoops. For twenty years he's worked on *Artful Dodge,* nursing it through the mimeograph runs of graduate school all the way up to a full-fledged national journal with staff and grants and a basement office and a logo (looks like a dead turtle—we'll have to talk).

So far, this is what being a poetry editor has meant: I go to the English Department and pick up a carton big enough for a Xmas tricycle, wrestle it out to the car, rope the trunk, schlep the box into my living room and tear the flaps off. Then I dig in.

Next comes the sorting. At first this felt slightly indecent: opening some-one else's mail and reading letters addressed, "Dear Dan," or "Dear Mr. Bourne," or "Dear Poetry Editor." And the letters themselves: everything from shoulder-padded university letterhead, spangled with credentials, to ticker tape "bios," to handwritten notes that drop out of the sheaf like a bizarro ransom note: "take me." Until now I've always been on the other side—wondering whether to enclose covers, what to say, how to entice without explaining, praise without fawning. Philip Dacey has written a grand "Form Rejection Letter," and William Trowbridge of *The Laurel Review* sends out a gem of a subscription renewal letter, complete with veiled threats from "Trigger Bob in the mailroom." In this vein, there ought to be a poem entitled "Form Cover Letter." Maybe I'll write it. Then I'll write a cover.

Poets often try to gauge editors' biases: for or against rhyme; political or pastoral; confessional vs. ironic; experimental or narrative. At this stage, I hold a mild grudge against every envelope I handle. When I sling a batch into the reject pile, I'm cheered. There's a small sense of achievement. Not because I'm glad to see bad poems or because I'm gloating that someone (even folks with muscled covers) could write such dreck. It's just that I'm a half-inch closer to finishing.

That's Pile 1. It's a happy pile. I unfold SASE, check postage, stuff poems and form letter, lick (piquing a delicious neurosis about poison), and place in Pile 1. Meanwhile the husk which contained the processed poems is marked "No," and placed in Pile 1-A to be checked later against submissions records. The process is clean (except for the lick) and certain. Progress is steady. Standards are confirmed. *Artful Dodge* needs these poems; they are the foundation upon which the journal rests.

Pile 1 is the most human pile. Most Pile 1 poems rely on two beliefs: (1) human experience has intrinsic value; and (2) this value can, should, and ultimately needs to be reported. This imperative is so strong that it sloshes over acquaintance; it outstrips instruction; even sex can't stem it. I think of Galway Kinnell's lines about his correspondence school students: "their loneliness / given away in poems, only their solitude kept." Somehow, only strangers can satisfy this human need to testify. This afternoon, I represent those strangers. I try to be gentle. I read the covers for clues, imagine the life from which the poems emerge. I read a little longer than is necessary to decide.

Pile 2 isn't a pile at all. It's a stack thick as a bankroll. These are the poems I'm going to live with for a while. They are about Gerald Cambriensis and the drift between days and nights; there are phloem and chrisoms, culvers, legerdemain.

These poems are hilarious, moving, compendious, eerie. Having torn them from an envelope, I feel as if I've assisted, if not at a birth, then at a baptism. These are poems I would have written if I'd been given the talent or vision or occasion. I read them out loud; I want to learn them by heart. Looking over Pile 2, I'm amazed how various the poems are. I don't see a pattern: lyric or dramatic, light or dark, formal or free. If these choices reveal my taste, I don't know what school I belong to.

What I learn from Pile 2 is how desirous we all are—even poetry editors—to be absorbed, how apt we are for transformation. Sure, I'm surly at first—having read so many submissions I feel like I'm being stoned with marshmallows. But when a Pile 2 poem comes, I feel it—sometimes from the very first line. I'm carried away; I trust implicitly the voice, suspending critical faculties. It might be oracular: "Out of the Rolling Ocean, the Crowd." Or startling: "My mother has your shotgun." Or serene: "I cannot think of anything today / That I would rather do than be myself." In every instance, there's a certain authority, the feeling of something impelled, not invented. Here are a few from Pile 2; see if they grab you:

> Elvis is reading the Bible to the scantily-clad girls
> Draped on his armchair.
> (Fleda Brown)

> I can plot Jupiter's elliptical orbit on a brown
> Paper bag using a protractor, ruler and pencil.
> (Adela Najarro)

> The Lord is a shepherd, he is eating the sheep.
> (Edward Bartok-Baratta)

> Nick
> said, "Don't worry, I won't
> ever die on you, OK?"
> and for a second I
> believed him.
> (Denise Duhamel)

Then there's Pile 3. There's absolutely nothing wrong with the poems in Pile 3. Pile 3 poems show craft; they exude professionalism; they demonstrate familiarity with tradition. Taken individually, these poems are capable of being admired. But there are so many. They create a mood that closes over you gradually, like a climate. It's heavy, Pile 3 is. It bulges. Each envelope is as spongy as blood pudding. Pile 3 offers up the kind of reading you do late at night when your thumb aches and you read three pages before you realize you've been rereading. If I were called in and asked to describe Pile 3 poems for the sketch-artist, here's what I'd say.

There were two of them, officer. They were narratives; there was a story, kind of, or at least a setting. One was outdoors, one indoors, I'm sure of that. Irony? Yes, I felt a bit. Tepid. They each wore two observations—like this; no, closer together. Everything was consecutive. Things floated toward a moral, implied: One was, "life, savor it." The other, "life, improve it." Or maybe "fuggetaboutit." They weren't workshop poems. They didn't bop in from the street, either. Syntax was normal. Loose lines—tetrameter maybe. One was enjambed, radically. The other read like a sentence with no parole. But it's hard to tell; the light was bad . . .

By the sixth inning Pile 3 starts to swell. Most Pile 3 poems believe they belong in Pile 2. Their postmarks snarl. Their covers prepare appeals. I know what they want. They miss their study with the banker's lamp and sofa. They miss the respect which came from the hard work that went into their making. They miss their names. Where else but here, in the first stage of editing a journal, would these poems be read without the protection and empathy provided by book jacket, classroom, or friendship?

When I hear, "Let thought become the beautiful woman," one word is absent: "Hafiz." When I read, "I have eaten the plums which you left on the refrigerator," what keeps the door ajar is the murmur, "Williams." Without those key words, these chestnuts might well have been headed for a long stretch in history's Pile 3. Am I cynical? Calling the great poets mandarins? No. But I'm afraid that certain poems might need a pinch of something, like "Emily." Maybe they need an approach supplied by history or critical prose. Maybe they need a better editor.

That's why there's Pile 4. Most Pile 4 poems did time in Pile 3. Some sounded so crazy at first they were committed to Pile 1. A few poems arrived here directly, often from long distances. How they made it I don't know. They won't say, even when I shake them. These poems hint at something beyond my ken. There are times I'm not sure Pile 4 poems are poems at all. Sometimes they come naked, with no cover, and I wonder if perhaps there hasn't been a clerical error. Maybe envelopes were exchanged? Maybe some clerk at the George Foreman Gas Grill and Metabolizer Warehouse is lip-reading: "It so happens I am tired of being a man." Not that I suspect Neruda of tampering from beyond.

As pleasurable as it is to come upon Pile 2 poems, I know that they aren't the ones that make a poetry editor. They are thoroughbreds groomed from the get-go; anyone could see that. Pile 4 is where a poetry editor makes his mark. Like a bird dog scout who glimpses the future star in the rank hayseed, a poetry editor needs canniness and patience to restore the envelope of silence that permits each poem to be fully heard. To handle Pile 4, an editor has to read every poem as if it were the first of the day—but not the first of his life. He has to follow poems fathoms deep, or through an aery clime, even though most often he's in for a nasty bump on the head. He has to remain able, against all odds, not only to discriminate among submissions, but to come under their sway.

Pile 4 also offers the best opportunities to exercise the poetry editor's prime function: to edit. A Pile 2 poem might permit some tinkering; but generally they are as clearly articulated as they are finely conceived. Pile 4 poems are often fixer-uppers. But it's important to be careful. Poets choose their editors—not merely by sending SASE. Before revising a poem, an editor should be committed to the body of the poet's work, so that when looking at an individual poem, he keeps in mind the poet's over-all vision. George Peffer writes that "the good editor tours the whole city before recommending changes." I'm loathe to roll up my sleeves. When I'm tempted, I remind myself that William Stafford hesitated to change his students' bad habits for fear that if cultivated, these very habits might yield originality. I also think here of Dan Langton, who used to say that the proliferation of poetry journals has caused the floor (Pile 1) to rise, but the ceiling (and maybe a few Pile 4 poems float up there) to come down. I think of my own leaky vessels sailing out there, while the nail in some poetry editor's mouth twitches.

At closing time Pile 4 has to fold. Everybody has to go home—back to 1 or 3. A few get the call to Pile 2. Then Pile 3 melts away. By night's end, there can be only two piles.

One of these days, Dan says, we're going to conference, compare notes, and put together the next issue. I can't wait. It will be something to see poems first loved on photocopy paper with their labels and signatures, headers, and "no stanza break" instructions, now dressed in *Antique Olive* and bound between the covers of *Artful Dodge*, number 38/39—a double issue.

Imagine them together in their plumage, flitting around the short stories, big as orchestral stands. What a ball. The fête swirls on; introductions are exchanged, champagne swilled, flirtations risked. I hope everyone likes each other. I hope it's the grandest bash since Gatsby. For me, lurking on a balcony, every single glittering guest is Daisy.

Letter to Bill Heyen

October 5, 2001

Dear Bill,

I have held off writing anything (thanks for asking), though the conversations are incessant, obsessive, and I wake up every morning and click the remote even now that they are down to interviewing compassionate restaurateurs and families who donated their penny jugs. The reticence comes from spending so long trying to be a poet—I think, "what would Yeats say?" when the media have replayed over and over the scene now marked on our collective psyche (and even as I write "psyche," my ears pop). For years I shied away from writing directly about anywhere in poems: Africa, Ireland, Manhattan, California. I layered every line to sift out the exotic. I didn't want to be a tourist (I went to graduate school, read theory). But what's left? I'm from Queens. Flushing. Fresh Meadows. St Kevin's Parish, the 111th Precinct. True, I lit out. I've been to Ujiji, where Livingston met Stanley, and to Oisin's tomb in the Antrim hills, where John Hewitt's cairn reads: "My Chosen Ground." I'm homesick for the world. I never go back to Queens, except to fly. The neighborhood's all changed—my brother drove by the ancestral row house and told me the Pucerellis were the last of the old crowd. I still fear Ronnie Pucerelli's windmilling fists. I remember when the twin towers were built. They got placed on every tour I gave to friends visiting New York, who mistook me for a guide. Sometimes my father went with us. But his New York was all rancor and nostalgia: Coney Island, the Botanical Gardens, the trattorias where mafia kingpins got hit. I did time in the Bronx. From Fordham, Manhattan seemed exotic as Khartoum. If I'd stayed, I might have gotten there. Others did. McGorry became a broker. Why not me? Or a fireman, like Vinnie Halloran. He was one of my brother's cronies—Duffy and Horan and Halloran, firemen all. Vinnie's big brother Terry was in my class. I haven't seen any of them since high school. I'm so sorry about Vinnie, and Marie, his widow, and the five kids. How can I say anything? The country is so vast that grief must be conducted via satellite; our horror packaged and desiccated (there I go) by the screen or page; I recoil from theory (honest reticence is rooted deeper—my business is circumference, says Dickinson). It's horrible that we're stuck with who we are, that we can't ululate or tear out our hair, burn effigies or flay skin. I feel awful about leaving Queens, as if my failure to woo Mary Ellen O'Brien in eighth grade, thereby not dating and subsequently impregnating and marrying her and raising kids in a duplex in Astoria, was the pivotal moment in my life and that of my ghost family. Are words more real? Or the ground I've chosen? Can a poem live up to the dead? I loved the e-mails from the Great Mother conference (bomb them with roses, send Shamans). I've shut up for decades, trying to be a poet. Yeats loomed, with all the ghosts "who converse bone to bone." I'm moving toward them now. Strapped in. Sometimes language takes off and I get that knot in the pit of my stomach, thinking: we will never land alive.

This Is Heyen Speaking

IN "THIS is Yeats Speaking," Charles Olson amps his fury against the mandarins who caged Pound by stealing Ben Bulben's thunder. Magisterial as Olson was—six-foot-eight not counting ghostly mantle—he hardly lacked brass; yet he styled his plea for Pound's release in the voice of Pound's patron. I love that essay, as I love Pound's own febrile allegiances—all but the last. In the postwar years of penitence granted to him by the intercession of friends living and dead, he slipped off to Italy, site of his most troubling entanglements. I picture him—the shock of white hair inches above his ormolu table—scribbling letters late into the night while his secretary, Desmond O'Grady, slipped in with cups of tea, hovering awhile the way Ezra perhaps once hovered, clerking for Yeats. Pound hardly slept in those Italian years, smiled seldom. This faint echo of history I overheard thirty years ago in a snug on Western Road in Cork, eavesdropping as O'Grady held forth over a crescent of small whiskies. And late last night I basked in that whisky-tinted memory when Bob Mooney phoned to read me Seamus Heaney's latest contribution to the *New York Review of Books,* a poem about a Boston fireman which had us chortling for the way it wedges ancient allegiances deep into the grain, describing the eponymous "Helmet" as "headgear / Of the tribe, as O'Grady called it"—thus celebrating not only an Irish-American firefighter, but also a slight *Selected Poems* that disappeared soon after its release from Gallery for £3.60, clothbound, in 1979. In the recitation's afterglow, I reminded Bob how my father would, post-whiskies, urge me to introduce myself to Seamus, since my grandmother is a Heaney from that parish. How easy to feel sometimes that we are all eavesdropping on familial echoes.

I don't need to whisper across spectral borders to conjure up William Heyen; his living voice is vibrantly its own. Yet I borrow his name and invoke his towering presence not just to praise work that grows in stature as it's shadow-fed, but also to affirm an engagement that grips from before and beyond. This year Heyen has published two books of poems, *Shoah Train* and *The Rope*, and though they are quite different in theme, they share allegiances to history, to earth, to Turtle Island, to Long Island, to childhood, and to book-making.

Start with the least allegiance first: despite a distinguished career, Heyen has chosen for his newest books two little-known publishers, Etruscan and Mammoth. I say "the least allegiance,'" but for Heyen, the making of books is no casual concern. His own extensive collection, gathered over forty years, has been ceded to the University of Rochester, where it graces the climate-controlled "Heyen Room." His recent essay, "Shredding," published in *Eclipse*, reveals his devotion to the book as a made thing, expressing his dismay at BOA's intended cost-saving practice of destroying overstocked titles. While his poems on Crazy Horse, the Gulf War, Ecology, the British Royals, and the Holocaust have scythed through world history, as for the books themselves, he nurtures each leaf with a gardener's touch, declaring, "I just want them to exist," and posting them one by one—these beautiful objects—from his cabin at the back of his property in Brockport, New York, where I picture him this morning, "surrounded by wild rose, honeysuckle, and red osier bushes," writing to say that he's sent *Shoah Train* "as far away as to Merwin under his Maui palms, to Zimmer under Wisconsin oaks and maples, to Bob Morgan along the Ithaca ravines of beech & ash."

What a morning, to receive by mail such a book! What affirmation that the nourishing word is "under your bootsoles" or beneath what cousin Seamus's "Helmet" calls "the crest" where you can almost taste "Tinctures of sweat and hair oil / ... the withered sponge and shock-absorbing webs" that provide our connective tissue to the dead.

Some might dismiss my praise of *Shoah Train* on the grounds that, with the nocturnal Mooney, I run Etruscan Press. For them, I stretch beyond my gangly height to say, "This is Heyen speaking." Mooney and I, along with Steve Oristaglio (if only you had known such bankers, Ezra), believe that thus we speak our mind, amplified, in the work we admire. When we decided to organize that sentiment into a nonprofit literary press, brainstorming a board of advisors who wore the headgear of the tribe, Bill Heyen was prime. On the morning of September 12, 2001, he reminded us why: phoning from Brockport with the idea to galvanize the energies of the American imagination into a response, attempting what Pound confessed finally that he had failed to do: make it cohere. From Heyen's labor—not merely of love but of anger and disgust and need and shock—emerged *September 11, 2001: American Writers Respond,* offering poetry and prose from one hundred twenty-seven writers.

Easy now to point to the lacquered crest of the elegant hardcover edition, to celebrate the tribal achievement, but in the weeks following 9/11, as Heyen circulated invitations to contribute to a book without antecedent from an unknown press, the prospects seemed less sanguine. To find detractors I don't need to cite, as Heyen does in both his introduction and later in *Shoah Train,* Theodor Adorno's famous declaration that "to write poetry after Auschwitz is barbaric," I merely recall one response to "The Dragonfly," a poem Heyen e-mailed to friends on September 11 and which I spread (too widely!) on September 12. "This is not a time for self-aggrandizement," wrote one list-serve recipient, "but for silent resolve. Shut the fuck up." This virulence hints at how unbridgeable is the rift between those who see poetic engagement in world events as "self-aggrandizement" and those whose balance between self and other is precarious, mediated by resonating, sometimes terrifying, echoes.

In *September 11, 2001: American Writers Respond,* contributor Bruce Bond posits the quandary that underlies Heyen's most recent books. "The challenge of all politically charged art," writes Bond, "is for the authority of the work to reside not merely in the given situation, charged as it is by ready-made pathos, but in the quality of spontaneous imaginative participation in that situation, what calls us to drag the newsreel to the recesses of the unconscious, to wed a passionate authenticity with expressive freedom." Bond releases the energy latent in that oxymoron, "political art," by splitting it, wedging in the word "charged"—in which I hear an echo of "responsibility" of the kind Yeats traced to dreams. Because such art does not parse us as individuals facing specific crises, it is not a call to action; but by the same stroke, the "charge" deflects the bromide that "poetry makes nothing happen," since it plumbs recesses where William Stafford's "justice," invoked by Heyen in the 9/11 introduction, "will take millions of intricate moves."

Such intricate justice requires what Heyen calls in an interview published in *Artful Dodge,* "a joyful equilibrium." It demands the negative capability to balance the ambition necessary to conceive responses to September 11, the Holocaust, or the fate of the planet, with the self-effacement to bookmark each slender volume of poems with a handwritten note, while imagining the trees shading the house where it will be received. Without such equilibrium, we know where ambition leads—to a cage in Pisa. This is the question that politically charged art (and not "identity politics," as it is commonly defined) is charged with: how to speak with an individual voice resonant with echoes. How to be the crest and the shock-absorbing webs?

Here is one such echo, from a poem in *Shoah Train* called "Testimonies, 1946":

> The German said for two people
> to fill a railroad car with coal
> and for two people to lie on the floor
> and be covered. When they were covered
>
> he laughed at us and ordered us
> not to dig them up, they should
> swim up by themselves, and if they cannot
> they can just stay there.

Entering these words on a screen, I find myself momentarily adrift between worlds, as if by transcribing I participate more fully in the testimony. Although I've read the poem many times, I hear now for the first time, for instance, how the act of witnessing is authenticated by idiom and inflection, and the way the poem is lineated to unshoulder "floor" on the doubled "covered" and "ordered," while "should" slaps up against "cannot." Even in reporting, Heyen remains uncomfortably aware of the complicity of art.

Yet, while noting the features of a powerful poetic statement, I know that such crafted testimonies by themselves may not distinguish *Shoah Train* from many other contemporary books of poetry on the Holocaust, such as Stephen Herz's *Whatever You Carry: Poems of the Holocaust;* Michael O'Siadhail's *The Gossamer Walls: Poems in Witness to the Holocaust;* and Lyn Lifshin's *The Blue Tattoo*—books which proffer witness in absentia. By themselves, perhaps such poems would not justify the unearthing and caging of these words in stanzas. But *Shoah Train* mediates a more complex set of relationships, based not only on individual witnesses, but also on the connections which thrum beneath, engulfing voices, poet, and reader.

Shoah Train is Heyen's third full-length collection on the Holocaust; his second, *Erika,* was a much-expanded edition of *The Swastika Poems,* released in 1977. Like *Erika, Shoah Train* bears testimony to Heyen's German ancestors, his Long Island childhood, his place as an American and a world citizen in the postwar era—and to concerns and presences which echo in the voices of witnesses, Nazis, ancestors, and dream figures that people these sequences.

In *Shoah Train*'s "Dedication, 1939," Heyen's grandfather, a German POW during World War I, receives a kiss on the cheek from Hitler. In "Chimney," his father, an immigrant who "smoked three packs a day and hid behind his smoke," offers a fiercely iambic, punctuation-stripped version of Adorno's Auschwitz dictum: "He didn't want to hear it what's the use." The father—no, not *the* father but William Heyen's father—is invoked, not to accuse or to ridicule, but as a presence to contend with: "He'd raise his hand, & threaten, but not hit." Such an indelible presence makes it necessary to broaden affinities—as Heyen himself conjures, in a poem called "Almond," his own presence:

> *"Herr Professor Doktor Heyen,*
> meine Name ist Maria Mandel,
> SS Auschwitz. I place myself here
> in your imaginings by free will . . .

Whose "free will," I wonder—the man addressed? The SS guard's? Or that of the poet looming behind the dramatic scene? All partake in a violent reconfiguration of identities. In "Fugue for *Kristallnacht*," Heyen traces the fault lines beneath a survivor's memories with his painstakingly accurate transcriptions: "Who will live / will die . . ." she says. In "The Bear," Heyen lilts an eerie lullaby:

> Was alone, was carrying her bear with her.
> Was alone, was carrying her bear with her.
> Was alone, was carrying her bear with her.
> Bear to counsel, comfort, & protect her.

recalling Randall Jarrell's "Protocols," while "Easter Morning," shaped like George Herbert's devotional "Easter Wings," demands of the Christian God: "Where is Your center / that is nowhere?" Like Jerome Rothenberg's *Khurban*, to which I see kinship, *Shoah Train* works "in the center that is nowhere," where sound, idiom, thought and poetic tradition braid "a passionate authenticity" with "expressive freedom."

Here, a further intricate move becomes necessary. To speak in the voice of victims may risk usurpation; but what of that far more difficult task of articulating evil without repudiating our shared condition or surrendering to the axiom that even Hitler was human, an approach that neutralizes one of poetry's primary powers: to curse. The order of curse I'm talking about here is, like praise, a kind of charm that invokes forces beyond or beneath our ken, as Heyen does in "Ars Poetica":

> I said to my friend
> I like writing
> in the crematoria,
> I mean cafeteria.
> That aberrant word
> had surfaced
> by way of sound
> & the same rhythm.

In aberrant words, in compacted phrases (who will live/will die) in fricative slaps (should/cannot), forces beyond the infinite fraction (I first typed *faction*) of our separate individuality are engaged; and it is these forces, which cannot be channeled by blood, nationality, or ideals, which finally authenticate. Such powers compel a poetic allegiance—a willingness to commit fully to the music and insight that prescience (what Heyen calls "wildness") yields. Poetic allegiance implies a transmutation of sound into vision, a willingness not merely to report voices, but also to embody them.

That this prescience has consequences can be seen from Heyen's essay, "Unwilled Chaos," published in *Writing and the Holocaust* in 1988. About *Erika*'s "Poem Touching the Gestapo," Heyen writes, "I have been afraid of my poem, but I have trusted it, in part, because I have not quite understood it. . . . Whoever [my speaker] is, he has taken Gestapo visions inside himself and gone wild with them." Heyen's speaker—his speakers, his selfhood, his ancestors, his enemies, his shadow—all blend in a wildness to which he commits fearful resources.

The problems endemic to writing poems about the Holocaust, or about any historical event, have less to do with the usurpation of a single voice than with the authenticity of poetic commitments. As Etheridge Knight says, "when the IRA sends JUST ONE, just one soldier / to fight with say the American Indians, then I'll believe them . . ." Ultimately, our ancestors cannot nourish until they pass through us—fathers, cousins, organizations, presses, ideologies, and nations (those shadow cathedrals)—coalescing in echoes, rhythms, sounds.

So, I partake more fully in *Shoah Train* because of *The Rope,* a book concerning the environment composed over the same years Heyen was writing *Shoah Train.* Like his earlier books on the environment, *Long Island Light* and *Pterodactyl Rose, The Rope* may seem at first to be tethered to a subject; but its sequences, like the concluding long poem, "Annuli," which delves into the poet's awakening to the natural world, range far. Located at the end of the millennium, facing possible extinction, *The Rope* also effaces time and distance—folding into eight lines, for instance, Thoreau, JFK, Yankee Stadium, and helicopters, all whorled within "insects / in whose intestines our Milky Way is one of countless / clusters in the eye of Time."

The maples, cherry blossoms, mute swans, ozone, tarballs, municipal incinerators, and yellow jackets which proliferate in *The Rope* shimmer in the ghostly figures from *Shoah Train.* Both books—like all of Heyen's poetry—echo in "that center that is nowhere" where no holocaust, no ecology, no history, no event, is not invested with inclusivity of the particular. Reading these lines from *The Rope*'s "Transcendentalism,"

> Early May, under a white oak, I broke open an acorn
> the squirrels missed. Already, its meat was filaments
> of mossy fibers within which struggled larvae
> of insects unknown to me . . .

I sense . . . not a correspondence—nothing that linear—but rather, a kinship with "Elegy" from *Shoah Train,* which cites Primo Levi's poem "Wooden Heart," and concludes by asking:

> but did the tree, *does* it still in living memory
> reach down into the covenant that every May
> bursts with these red-streaked white blossoms?

In these entwining roots, outrage at the Holocaust is tinged with despair at the coarsening of the atmosphere—each particle and universe partaking in "joyful equilibrium" so that no poem calcifies or bloats on subject or ego. This is the project ("move it on, instanter, citizen," says Olson in his own twang). We abide in wildness: in and with and through, fully engaged, yet separate, down to the cellular and syllabic levels.

Perhaps this is what finally confounded Pound in Pisa when he wrote, "I cannot make it cohere." Perhaps he could no longer make himself cohere, could no longer bring his enormous intellectual faculties to bear on the disparities of scale with which his *Cantos* and his life contended. It was no failure of talent or will or design. Maybe he could no longer balance the great with the small, as he had done so brilliantly throughout his life—revisioning the history of China, then rummaging in the closet to send Joyce a pair of secondhand boots.

No, I burden him unfairly, *il miglior fabbro,* to judge now. This I hear, distinctly, but not directly, from Dante's lips.

My Dinner with Joe

JUST AS in the movie, I arrive first. The host swishes through a candlelit archipelago to my reservation behind a potted palm. Before I've deconstructed my napkin, a frocked waiter materializes. I don't recall Wallace Shawn's drink, but I book a Beefeaters straight up. When Joe rolls in, I duck around the plant to greet him. In the mood light, he does look like Andre Gregory—maybe an Italian version—leather and indigo, though to me he'll always be the frizz-headed kid I met thirty-five years ago. Since then we've been a few times around the block, and though our roads forked, we've remained close, glimpsing in each other reflections of unlived possibilities. I'm in New York for a poetry reading. Joe's here for a job interview in the private sector after twenty years grinding for the CIA. It all feels stagy—crossing paths at the nexus of two worlds—but whatever our CVs claim, we're still two jocks from Queens.

Besides the martinis, tonight's menu features a special: *A Poetic/ Political Discourse* moderated by National Book Award finalist H. L. Hix. Titled *God Bless,* it's a book of poems composed entirely of clips from the speeches of that great American poet, George W. Bush, pitted against interleaves from the Islamic laureate, Osama bin Laden. Hix contends that since the principals won't poke their psyches out of Oval Office and

Afghani cave to face off, they'll have to duke it out here. I sent Joe *God Bless* because he loves this stuff; while his days were spent pinning flags on maps, in the evenings he'd grab a beer and riffle through the last three decades of American poetry. But this book's different from the tomes on Joe's bookshelves, and different too from Hix's other works—an eclectic range of poetry, criticism and philosophy. It's shaken me up, and as for Joe, well, he's no neo-con, but he takes verse the way I take martinis.

Looking up from the wine list, Joe shrugs: "No maison de la ferme de boone?"

"Yeah, some joint," I roll my eyes.

Before we get to the main event, the proprieties must be observed. There's the NBA playoffs, Joe's son's soccer tourney, gossip from old pals, our latest injury reports, a few jokes.

Cradling a bottle labeled with a griffon rampant on a grape cluster, the waiter reappears, bends an inch, and uncorks. Joe winks at me, giving the Pharaoh's nod; two ruby goblets are poured.

With the second glass of nostalgia, we get down to it.

"So, what do you think of Hix's latest?"

Joe steeples his fingers; his tanned brow furrows.

"You know I love his books," he begins. "*Chromatic* is jazzed—the poems really move, but they feel grounded too: there's a story just underneath the surface, even if I don't always get the thread. How about 'Eighteen Maniacs'? All those funky handles: Dizzy, Cheraw, Shaw nuff, Coloratura. I'm not sure who's who—it feels like walking a city street, getting an intense hit off each passing face." Joe's arm stiffens, leading a fast break. "Like the man says, 'Watch expectantly to see precisely what is here. / Listen expectantly to hear precisely what is not.'" He leans forward, planting his elbows. "Remember his reading in that basement dive in the Village?"

"Cornelia Street Cafe."

"The poem about the dying woman whose husband is hearing voices?"

"Prelude and Fugue."

"No way you'd know that from the text—but it's there all the same, underneath. I sense it, anyway. And villanelles embedded in the paragraphs? Make it new, baby."

I conjure a strange image: Dick Vitale meets Ezra Pound.

"But *God Bless*," Joe shakes his head. "These poems sound . . . well, they sound like Bush. And he ain't no poet."

Joe swirls his glass of Chianti. "I was thinking about the great political poems from Vietnam," he says. "Remember Robert Duncan's 'Uprising?'" Joe cants his head and raises a fork, going into hypnodrive: "'. . . and the very glint of Satan's eyes from the pit of the hell of America's unacknowledged, unrepented crimes that I saw in Goldwater's eyes . . .'"

Joe's fork taps anapestic time.

"'Now shines from the eyes of the President, in the swollen head of the nation.'"

It defies age, Joe's memory. Rap sheets, hoops stats, rock star bios, or poems: he always has it on the tip of his tongue. Legacy of a geeky childhood.

"And Bly," Joe exclaims. "'The Teeth-Mother Naked at Last'? 'The politicians lie, the ministers lie, the professors lie, the television lies. What are these lies? They mean that the country wants to die.'" Joe shuts his eyes, his fork beckoning for a raggedy chorus: "'Do not be angry at the president, he is longing to take in his hand the locks of death hair.'"

Just off Joe's elbow, a buttery shoulder glimmers over sequins. On my left, a snifter floats under a profile the Brits could mint. There are a lot of reasons to love New York, but one of the best is that two guys cantilating poems with enough hand gestures to land a 747 don't draw a glance from tables inches away.

"They went past accusation, those poems. They don't point a finger, 'the President lies—or in this case, the President is an idiot.'" Joe says. "The lies and the idiocy are there in all of us. Bly knew that. They go beyond politics because they try to account for evil and stupidity."

He's on a roll now; I keep an eye on his forehead. We call it "the vein": when it throbs, Joe's close to postal.

"Bly and Duncan understood that their personal identities were this—" Joe snaps his fingers. "Their forms felt energized because they came from something deeper than the personal. Feet in clay, ear to the wind."

"Well," I say, snapping into prof-mode. "You've seen Hix's interview at the end of *God Bless*. The poets of the sixties worked against the conventions of that time, he says: the stump speech and sermon. Their long, biblical strophes one-upped political speeches. New forms emerge from the constantly changing culture."

Listening to myself, the voice sounds thin. Has thirty years of lecturing chalked my throat? I knock back a mouthful, feel the resin coarsen my fiber, and carry on.

"The poet's a lightning rod—channeling the flow. We don't hear sermons or stump speeches anymore. It's a postmodern climate, a different kind of critique. *God Bless* strips us down to who we are: receptors in a media-saturated world."

"OK," says Joe, tearing a sesame roll. "But the approach—is it new? Sounds like us versus them. You can dress it up in theory. But if this is meant to spark political debate, then why put it in lines? Why not call it satire and run it in *The Onion*?"

"You're right. It's more than satire," I reply. "It's not just politics."

I top off our rough red.

"Joe," I say, gaining steam, "Isn't it weird that 9/11 and your war on terror haven't produced any cultural shift—no new artistic expression? Not that there hasn't been a lot written—the Web sites are all blogged out. But mostly it's just a reaction: screams and whines, the flip side of the pablum from the White House. Nothing new—no new vision that lets us see things fresh, the way Modernism was born from the trauma of World War I and postmodernism and the Beats followed World War II, and Rock went psychedelic during Vietnam. It's great that you've remembered those lines from Bly and Duncan—and I know you've got a whole cabal tickling the underside of that scalp, but there's a lot to forget too. What about the bombast? You know, 'Blood leaps on the wall . . .'? 'The death-bee is coming'? It gets awfully humid. And if they were so humble, then what's with the flowery vests?"

Joe's eyes roll, his patience wearing thin. "What do you mean, *my* war," he snarls. "I'm well out of it now."

It's so familiar, these contests. Seems like they've been going on since Stonehenge was a rock garden.

"Where's the new approach?" I push ahead anyway. "Rap music? Language poetry? They seem more and more disengaged. Hix is trying something new; and all new art feels raw at first. He's just, you know, 'cleansing the doors of perception.'"

"Doors of perception, huh." Joe reaches across the table and plucks off my specs. "Do you ever cleanse these?" He dips the filmy lenses in ice water and polishes with his napkin.

"Anyway, I hear the steak's good here." He thumbs the parchment menu.

It's not for the steak that people comes to places like this; it's for the improv. The violin musak, the faux-Italian china, the ceiling fan blades moving slow as clipper ships; they're all part of a set featuring ever-changing characters. The chefs are stage hands; the host directs; the waiters play bit parts, cued to enter when the conversation flags.

Joe doesn't make entrances easy. When he snaps the menu shut, the waiter moves in, but Joe freezes him with a referee's arm-pump. "New means of expression, huh? Well, quoting Bush out of context—that's a flagrant 2. Ten game suspension."

I grin at the stunned waiter and scan the calligraphy, spotting an old weakness, cherrystone clams.

"Calamari," Joe lilts, making it sound like Hix's nineteenth maniac.

"Why shouldn't poets take a stand in your real world?" I continue. "Neruda does, and Yeats, and Milosz, and Soyinka." Just saying the names sends a thrill down my spine. "Speaking against injustice doesn't compromise their art. And they name names: United Fruit, Parnell, Gdansk, Mugabe.

"Anyway, isn't that what Hix is up to?" I ask, crossing my dribble. "What you're saying about transitory identity? Getting out of himself, giving over to the givens. Not his words, but Bush's—which, whether we like it or not—are always in our heads. This is the ultimate surrender: Hix becomes what we all hear but never really hear."

"Except that these givens," retorts Joe, "are Hollywood-shallow. They don't break through." He chops the air. "Hix doesn't knuckle under to Bush—even I know that's what you guys call subtext. It's a jump ball. Bush's words versus Hix's intent. And it's a quick step from shuffling lines to slander. Do you know what I'd sound like diced up? Or you? Christ, you're stiff enough uncut."

Between us, a crumb-flecked linen tablecloth; two sauce-stained plates. A cocktail fork pricks a tiny liver-shaped heart of clam.

"And how come bin Laden doesn't get the same treatment?" Joe asks. "He winds up sounding a lot better than Bush—not that that's hard. What does Hix say, 'arguments *replicated from* . . . ?' Why not quote him straight—toss in the anti-Semitic drivel and the melodrama—did you hear the one about 'there will only be neck-biting between us.' Christ. Neck-biting. I don't know if you realize this, Romeo, but bin Laden's no Che Guevera. Even among the radicals he's a loose canon. What did Khalid Sheikh Mohammed say? 'It's a pity bin Laden has no intellect?'" Joe shrugs. "He and Bush are a good match."

By now the waiter's found his rhythm. His chevroned sleeve floats to refill glasses; his notepad is cocked and poised. I steer clear of the unpronounceables. Porterhouse, rare. Joe looks up, heaves a sigh. Tuna nicoise salad. It's the blood pressure—plus the fact that Saturday mornings he still hobbles up court with guys half our age, though his knee cartilage is thin as an alibi. Or maybe he's still chewing on "Uprising," which recalls, "the fearful hearts of good people in the suburbs turning the savory meat over the charcoal burners and heaping their barbecue plates with more than they can eat."

"Funny thing," says Joe, stabbing a brown tentacle. "*God Bless* reminds me a little of what I was leaving behind in the Agency."

"How's that?" I ask, taking the bait.

"Well, we lurk, Hix and us." Joe unrolls his collar, miming a spy. "By the way, where's Hix these days?"

"Wyoming."

"Whew." Joe's eyes scan windswept buttes.

"But I mean poetry and espionage. Lots of cache, not much pub—when things are going well. We both use codes. It's all about indirection, nuance. But in this book, Hix comes out straight—the way we had to after the WMD affair. And you see where that leads."

I take a sip, hold the glass globe steady in the air. Prismed in syrupy light, Joe's face swells, contracts. We're not young, even looked at straight. In high school, Joe once leapt out of a classroom window when the priest's back was turned. Now, he's like a city block seen from a rooftop: the gridded thrum. And as for a plotline, it's blunt as a highway dash. Wife, children, and now a high-stress career, dead-ended.

The waiter swivels toward us, one arm tawny and the other emerald. We lean back to make room. With a flourish, he pilots the platters down. "Don't touch," he whispers to me. "Plate's hot." Though it didn't burn him.

Joe's salad glints with oiled peppers, tomatoes, egg slices, and ribbons of fish. My baked potato yawns steam; broccoli stems sweat beads of lemon. The steak covers two zip codes. A second waiter initiates the liturgy of the pepper shaker, followed by the ceremony of awe, in which we all join, conducted with nods and smiles, until both waiters withdraw. Silence descends as Joe and I address our separate fortunes.

As I worry the bone's nape and Joe forks lettuce, my mind wanders over a star-strung skein of evenings: pub grub at The Deer Park, bottomless National Bohemians at Dunkels, tranquil pints in Ballydehob, sessuins in Youngstown, belly dancers in London, *Haute Cuisine* in Montpelier, Chianti classico in Tuscany, palm wine in Kolwezi, saki in Osaka. Yet, I can't connect the dots. What year was this night? When that one? Unlike Joe, whose days and nights are wound taut, my memories flash randomly, a highlight film of a game never played.

"I don't blame you guys for the WMD mix-up." I say, as the prandial mood dissolves. "Oedipus didn't know either."

"Hey, lay off the knitting needles," Joe grins.

"Joe, remember that think tank you were in a few years ago? They told you, 'Think way, way outside the box.' What did you come up with? 'Bin Laden's delegating more. He doesn't need to attack America again.' Duh. Who couldn't figure that out? But there were people out there who did know. I remember one guy—Appleman was his name. This guy's a professor in some midwestern school. Doesn't have access to a decent bagel much less classified intelligence. But he had bin Laden's strategy down cold. Wrote a piece in that book I sent you, *September 11, 2001: American Writers Respond.* I still remember it."

I deploy my knife to count greasy fingers.

"*One.* America must be destroyed, and we can't do it ourselves. We have to get the whole Muslim world worked up. But how? Attack America, so that, *Two...*" Here I tap blade on middle finger. "... America strikes back, killing thousands of Muslims ... and *Three,* a whole generation of Muslims rises up against the US.

"The 9/11 book didn't sell that well, but it wasn't top secret. You could have passed your copy on to your pals and saved us a few wars."

"Sure," Joe snorts, pushing back his chair, "A million Monday-morning quarterbacks. Be right back."

I sip, and let my gaze wander around the restaurant. Every table is occupied; each party enthralled in its own world. A triumvirate in gunmetal gray conspire; a straight couple purrs, so frilled they must be back from a tango lesson. A divorced father passes a wicker basket filled with guilt and longing, disguised as bread, to his fey daughter. Each drama is so singular that they all seem the same; they've taken on the gilded tint of passersby coasting by the stenciled glass logo.

Often, walking Manhattan streets, I glimpse a familiar face I can't place until I realize it's an actor—I've seen the face in commercials or on sitcoms. In this city, Hix's "Doggin," "Tickle Joe," "Intervallic," and "Klackto-veedsedstene" rub shoulders with those of us still seeking names.

Joe weaves back. Before he reaches his seat, I'm all over him.

"This is why *God Bless* isn't just political satire. You have to read the lines as Bush, then read them again as poetry. This gulf opens up between the banal things Bush says, like, 'We need more power, pure and simple, / to make . . . the world a more peaceful place' and what we want from poetry. The chasm is the message: we're faced with a vast emptiness. Hix doesn't tell you what the emptiness means. It's yours; you have to create your own meaning.

"For me, when I read Bush condensed and patterned, it's like reading his brainwaves. It becomes apparent he wants no part of a certain kind of human experience that has always been poetry's métier—what we've called the unconscious. Bly and Duncan tried to get there directly, through incantation, deep image, and appeals to a sense of community, and of course rich language. But it's different now. We don't share the same stories anymore; we can't follow the same path. It's as if we're all bouncing around like random atoms. You say Hix is being transparent. But he's not: when you read *God Bless* you're also seeing in forms—the villanelles, sonnets, odes—shadows of the poems you've loved in the past. And they're not here now—maybe not even possible—and what's closing them off is this chatter, this empty chatter, that's all around us.

"That's why this is new, and has to be new. You can't follow Bly down the stairs as if he's Dante. You're on your own. And some people don't want to go down the stairs at all. And suddenly you understand why Bush avoided the cave. Even when he talks about bin Laden, he has to talk from a safe distance, using religious cant—'evildoers'—or Western TV slang—'dead or alive.' But what he can't talk about is his own fear of the dark. So he attacks Saddam, a mirror image, a false king who attacked his father."

"Thanks, Doc," says Joe. "But in your world, where the seminar never sets, it's easy to analyze. You get it wrong, so what? You've still got tenure. Nobody dies. But where I live—where we all live except you, Plato—it's one shot and you're done. You think that doesn't make your hand shake?"

"Isn't that built into any institution?" I ask. "Po-biz is as fraught with intrigue as the CIA, even if nobody gets killed. What if any system—no matter how weighty or fragile—can't get it right, because it's unable to extricate itself from itself? Forget Oedipus, you're like Laocoon strangled by snakes. Didn't matter that Laocoon knew the horse was hinky, he couldn't find a way to untangle himself from institutional thought. The committee mind: it's a nest of snakes, pulling you down.

"That's why Hix had to break free from his own snakes—the expectation that poetry is beautiful and complicated and arcane. He had to wrestle loose from Bly with his shaman vest and mystical Duncan. Away from a codified poetry that everyone admires and no one reads."

"Sure," says Joe. "He wants to be original. Wants to be new. That's what pulls us down: our desire to be different. To be seen. We wind up caught right here," Joe taps two wine stains on the linen, "in the here and now.

"You want new forms—new ways to approach this crisis?" he asks. "Why? So you have something new to teach? I don't need poetry to show me why I can't escape. I want poetry to free me from the illusion of being separate. Because the truth is—and we're blind to it—we're all versions of one another. Bush doesn't see this, so he winds up attacking his own reflection rather than facing the figure in the cave. Hix doesn't see it, so he separates himself from his own poetic power to face Bush.

"You say God Bless reveals the power of poetry and the vapidity of Bush by cleansing perception, showing that we've been duped by a veneer of poesy. You say that if the new poem is depressing, that's because it reveals an ugly truth. But poems that live on the surface—even if the surface is shadowed—just drain capital: eating away at our expectations that poetry might offer sacred insight. Let's face it, there's enough bad verse out there without a genius adding to it.

"I'm holding on to the belief that poetry can offer something else. Something that stays while everything else changes—our identities, our selves. Otherwise it's all a shell. What holds the past and present together is . . ." Joe's hand searches the air. "Unsayable," he says. "That's what those snakes are: the unsayable. They're always there. Always the same. If we resist them—if we don't hear them—we'll never shed our skins. We need to listen, not wrestle.

"Think about it. Imagine you tried to take this evening home." Joe's gaze takes in the room. "All this talk: what you said, what I said. You script it out. You get all the details. You even look up all the poems we couldn't quite remember so we sound better.

"And what if you went a step further—and described the whole scene: this stupid plant." Joe plucks a frond spear, and waves it toward the adjoining table. "The babe in the blue dress." He flicks the stem on the floor. "And the crumbs on your lapel." He reaches over and swats my jacket.

"You could even make a movie," Joe offers. "Like the one with those two Manhattan guys at dinner—no plot, no other characters. One of them goes on about escaping the world by dancing with nymphs and faeries, and the other wants his *Daily News* and coffee.

"You could plot out the space between these two guys, the way *God Bless* measures the gulf between idioms—or is it idiots. But what about the vaster space inside?" Joe brushes his hand across his dark shirt. "What you can't get is the feeling of Duncan's lines coming through me—not caring who I seem, who I am. It's like driving to the hoop, everything slowing down, patterns coming into focus. None of that would be in your account. Sentences can't say that. Not polemics, not satires, not movies. It's only when you completely let go of identity that that stuff gets in.

"You know, that think tank? It didn't work because we were boxed into a notion of who we were. You can't break that habit in a month. You can't teach people to write outside the box, and return to the box every two weeks for a paycheck. That's what jobs do to us: close us in till we crack, and lose whole parts of ourselves. You talk about Laocoon. What we were missing was the Sybil. We didn't need an English prof's lecture; we needed some crazed woman in a cave speaking in tongues. We've lost that part of ourselves—the crazy, unsayable part. Hix has been to the cave and spoken to that crazed woman. And instead of going there now, he decides to stand up for himself against George Bush—same way Bush stood up against Saddam."

The restaurant's starting to empty out. We're reached the stage when my belly's gone global and my feet are asleep. Somehow, the set has changed. The sequins have vanished, and so has the English nobleman. Reflections flit across the plate glass. A decanter of Calvados has appeared before me, as if unbidden. Joe sips coffee stiffened with sambuca.

I feel unmoored, wondering how many nights we'll have, Joe and I, to be on stage together, wondering if we'll always be pushing back, if the pattern will ever be revealed.

"What was that John Cage line?" Joe asks. "'What we require is silence. But what the silence requires is that we go on talking.'" He shrugs, "Maybe Hix just wanted to come out of the cave for once. Just to be seen for himself, one man in the light. The thing is, Hix can go back. I can't."

On the cab ride home, the streets glisten to sepia, just as they did in the movie. The conversation jumbles in my head. Hix, Oedipus, Bush, Joe, Laocoon. The faces and phrases soften to a whisper: "In far Wyoming a poet leaves a cave, walking toward Queens, where Delphi commands a summit between Bush and his exiled id."

I strain my neck to peer at the countless lit windows above. Easy to lose myself, chauffeured through images of a native city I've never really lived in. Passing a silent breach, I sense the presence of the absent twins.

The vaster space inside. I close my eyes, let the towers rise pristine. But I can't hold them. Other images crowd in, enclosed in a screen: flames and swelling dust, crowds fleeing, a close-up of an anonymous face, screaming. It's the horror slide show of televised reality.

Do we need a different kind of art to cleanse the doors of perception?

Or does each freshly minted stratagem—the aesthetic equivalent of trendy restaurants and theatrical postures—merely clog the ancient passageways between lightning-rod skyscrapers and subways rumbling goat speech underground?

And what about Joe, slouched at his desk under fluorescent light, feeling lost, trapped in the here and now?

I think of the ancient Athenian general who, after failing to protect the city of Amphilos from the Spartans, was sentenced to exile in the city that had defeated him. Living among his enemies turned out to be no punishment; instead, it opened his eyes and led him to compose his great histories. "My work," wrote this disgraced general, known to us as Thucydides, "is not a piece of writing designed to meet the taste of an immediate public, but was done to last forever."

I pray, under the penumbra of these spectral towers, let H. L. Hix return to the muse's cave. Let Joe find a Spartan haven. Let us elude—or as Joe would say, 'hear'—the serpents gripping our flesh.

The Elsewhere

A Verse Essay

One summer solstice long ago I drove
northwest all night in the wavering
ether of highways beyond the Bronx,
rocketing past dormant satellites—
Yonkers, Hackensack, Newburgh,
approaching escape speed near Poughkeepsie,
glimpsing on dread cliffs impossible
flashes—meteors, spacecraft, even
houses perhaps breeding alien lives—
the inexorable randomness so frightening
I hurtled ever faster into the void.
Flight, yes; but no mortal pursuit—
only a fanatical faith in *hereness*
somewhere, triangulated between
accelerator and moon, a cosmic chi
exhaled as Pall-Mall smoke encoding
the energy-mass equation of *this, now*.
At last, near dawn, stars capsized,
I churned gravel coming to myself

at the double helix gate. Yaddo.
Prime Spondee. Planet of Lawn,
Honeysuckle and Turrets.
I shouldered the Ford Galaxy door open,
shielding my eyes against dilating light.

"Take two clocks and place against your ears,"
the palsied laureate declared. "Then,
separate by millions of light years."
Benchpressing chunks of air to his tufted skull,
he grinned and rolled his eyes, then wheezed,
"Each ticks slower than the other."
This was my first dinner at the mansion
under the chandelier nebulae
and the gold-leaf firmament of the sponsoring dead,
and truth is, for days the theorem held.
Dawn's event horizon splashed my face,
led me meandering down the hall,
past candlesticks and gargoyle figurines
to my West House garret studio,
where Roth, they said, had once committed *Portnoy*.
Zodiacs scarred the massive plank desk.
The spavined couch was sticky with stale zeal.
But in my cramped head space, squinting
through quarky gloom into the blip
of a primitive curser, I caught, almost, non-
zeroness: one and one and one. At two,
inertia chuffed me out, lunchpail in fist,
to lurk in an octagon pavilion plaqued
"Donation of Helena Hampton-Smythe."
Beyond the penumbra of entwining limbs,
rhythmic thwocks and tips of a lime parabola
radared a clay tennis court where
collared white angles intersected.
Once, an aura of forsythia and starpower
glided by my perch and I gulped,

"How's your day?" She half-turned,
eyes pooling into the middle distance,
and her lips moued as she uttered, "Bittersweet."
Then back to my capsule in the dying sun
to brood on the aqua screen until
I splashed down into paralytic nap,
deskness bonding with isotopes of drool.
Whatever I scanned reawakening
those deep evenings: cricket gurgle,
sleep-pocked cheek, fireflies
constellating in the windowbox—
all coalesced just as the laureate
had prophesized: waving his fork in time,
chanting that the spaced-out mind
must pluck from eleven strings a single
past, future and the intervals
composing all that isn't either.
Let five beats, I croaked into the moon-
lit sliver between *then* and *soon*,
monitor the frequency of *this now*.
Let this cell on this sublunary
childless tycoon's artist retreat estate
be the balloon of the expanding universe.
I inhaled ions, exhaled eons thus:

Midnight on Patrick's Bridge, I'm peering down
into the River Lee's drowned stars until
the thump of a Jersey pothole clenches my brain-
stem, triggering an El Cerrito
bar brawl that goes non-linear, plunking
the vapor trail of a little league fastball
tailing into my first, tentative
hard-on whence my father, dense
with matter, storms like a quasar
incarnating into Brooklyn,
curving space-time into a quick-

silver of humanoid history
thickening with geologic torpor,
Pangaea balled, the Antarctic
sucking Alaska's toes, morphemic soup
unrhyming into static to the always
that Plancked into the dying universe.

What's more seductive than the mantra *thnow*?
Even in the light years since those nights
it hums faint though when I crane
into the mirror and face age,
time shifts in parallax. Missing
thnow, my lifeline hugs the shore
like a mariner bereft of longitude,
or a spaceman pressing his nose to the earthward pane.
But Yaddo those first nights transmuted
particles and waves into present
sounds penetrating all. I scrolled
up and entered bold caps
cribbed from the laureate's hypnotic fork:
THE ELSEWHERE. Neither now nor when,
consequence-bereft, uncircumscribed
by past and future cones, the infinite
fraction between synapses and stars.
Out there beyond my portal, the world
stayed flat; scale insisting to the nth—
despite the post-modernist composer
scribbling all hours on the Steinway.
Summer ticked two beats past
zenith, Orion tilted declination,
and the pond thickened with crocuses and musk.
Whole days I lost, scuffling keds
through brambly curliques or dopplering
my Galaxy past moribund stables.
On the garlanded thoroughfare of Saratoga,
I slipped unseen among the equine

tourists preening by sleek watercolors.
In the neon-Irish sawdust-floor shebeen,
I curled into a booth sucking a pint
and stole peeks at Skidmore breasts and legs.
After a week of orbiting I finally cracked
open the oak door of the Mansion Parlor
where post-prandial junior residents
clustered around fame-fed fireballs.
"I know, out there," the Brahmin eco-
justice performance poet yawned,
stretched on a Chesterfield and gesturing
beyond the leaded glass, "Joyce and Shelley
are just a pair of Jersey cocktail waitresses."
In a globe-lit corner, surrounded by a crown
of 18th century fauteuil, the laureate
vibrated a forefinger, declaiming,
"As Homer once said," and his voice sank,
"I'm just going to read two poems."
For all Time's stringing out of Space
I still, for instants, seem diverse, therefore
those evenings prism to me now, the retina
wrestling to reverse the world, transmit
into *thnow*. But *thnow* siphoned
into syllables no longer thrums but spins
into the singularity *as if.*

One sleepless midnight two weeks into Yaddo
I stamped up the warped stairs to my studio
and fiddled my horsehead key into the lock.
No moon, no fireflies, no stars, no sound.
I probed with splayed fingers but the string
to the unglazed lightbulb eluded and
I leaned too far and funny boned
the phantom desk, sending dark
matter fractaling. Yipping, I slunk out,
as I slink now through another dark *as if*

melting immeasurable hours. Next
morning, after mansion tea and scones,
I climbed to face the moonscape. Legless,
the monolith stood upended: one flank
henged the floorboards, another hewed
the window's plaster nape. A crater
loured over a spew of drafts and notes
and the crashed unblinking craft of the laptop.

Change may take epochs but it is not slow.
That morning, free from covalent bonds,
I split the couch at the vortex of smoke gyres
and surveyed—nothing. The Elsewhere
was not yet a poem; it was whatever
flowed in all directions beyond flight.
But when the clocks resynchronized
after the crash at Yaddo, The Elsewhere—
like every line graphed on this page and all
the poems encrypted through the years—
massed slowly, cooling to lambent spheres
that loom in the night sky but remain
always ineluctably somewhere else.
Reentry into dying time began
the moment I glimpsed a mildewed pad
half-buried in the rubble. Digging it out,
I unstuck the gluey weft and thumbed a text
vestigial from some ancient residence.
It lies beside me now,
this fossil from a past beyond my past,
and opening it thrills, but can't erase
distances first charted that morning
when I sat cross-legged and uncreased
abandoned couplets, haiku, axioms,
networked in a riot of vectors
esoteric as Big Apple subway maps.
Midway through, dog-eared, and hyped

with gargantuan violet clouds I found
THE ELSEWHERE: Poem Past Rhyme or Sine.
On the next page, in miniscule block print,
If earth were made of a single atom
the nucleus would be smaller than this room.
Three more blank pages, then
the title reprised, this time wreathed in graphite
flames, spawning a new genesis
Poetry=physics, but selecting
words for a poem is just stamp-collecting.
More blanks. Then **THE ELSEWHERE** again,
enmeshed in equal signs, resulting in
Inside me mushroom 30 H-bombs.
My mouth can't even make a sound.
Throughout the rest of the composition tab
the sequence spluttered to start again and again
under the title constantly renewed
in pointillistic letters or wavy script.
Finally, it comet-trailed in Flair to the last draft:
I feel the presence of the past and future
but can't make The Elsewhere cohere.
And underneath, bridging a fissure
in the withered inside flap, a date
twenty-seven years before my time
above the barely legible autograph
of the man who would become the laureate.

So the last weeks passed and the residency
which began in epic flight ended with me
placing in the Yaddo ping-pong tourney
and making the rounds of Skidmore dorms.
Winched up, refurbished, and rescrewed,
the great plank desk bore my elbows
groanlessly every morning and the ultra-
musty ozone of the studio
bore into my brain as lines and stanzas

millimetered forward even as far
as this but never reaching *thnow*.
I didn't return the notebook, never spoke
to its author's incarnation as the laureate,
though zoning out during his chautauquas
or watching his knock-kneed shuffling at dusk
through the rose garden, I imagined
clocks fissioning from his ears and wondered
what he was, adrift from The Elsewhere,
wandering through Yaddo, winding down
one by one by one to nearly nought
even as the opus the world filed
under the heading *Deathless Verse*
emitted from his cloud-ringed cerebrum.

The pod I breathe in now feels absolute.
Space bears down on the winter sky
and my fingers slur over keys to enter *this*
now even as it burgeons and
divides. Beyond, the laureate
takes his place among the planets
Shelley, *Joyce*, and *Homer* fading to
the furthest coordinate bought on Name-A-Star.
My ungloved hand counts down from five
as if *thnow* could be reconciled. Before
zeroing out, I fumble to number-crunch
the hours when The Elsewhere seemed margined,
though it takes almost forever to cohere,
and an instant to extinguish, just like life.

Bibliography

Berlin, Irving. "Irving Berlin's Insomnia." *New Yorker,* August 26, 1996.

Bidart, Frank. *Stardust.* New York: Farrar, Straus and Giroux, 2005.

Bly, Robert, ed. and trans. *Selected Poems of Neruda & Vallejo.* Boston: Beacon, 1976.

———, ed. *The Winged Energy of Delight: Selected Translations.* New York: Perennial, 2004.

Bond, Bruce. *Cinder.* Wilkes-Barre, PA: Etruscan Press, 2003.

Brady, Philip. *Forged Correspondences.* Binghamton, NY: New Myths Press, 1996.

———. *Fathom.* Cincinnati: Word Press, 2007.

———. *To Prove My Blood.* Ashland, OH: Ashland Poetry Press, 2003.

———. *Weal.* Ashland, OH: Ashland Poetry Press, 2000.

Cavafy, C.P. *Collected Poems.* New York: Harcourt Brace, 1961.

Clements, Arthur L, ed. *John Donne's Poetry.* 2nd ed. New York: Norton, 1990.

Daniels, Jim. *Punching Out.* Detroit: Wayne State University Press, 1990.

Forche, Carolyn. *The Country Between Us.* New York: Harper & Row, 1981.

Ford, Patrick K, trans. *The Celtic Poets: Songs and Tales from Early Ireland and Wales.* Belmont, MA: Ford & Bailie, 1999.

Friel, Brian. *Selected Plays.* Washington DC: Catholic University Press, 1986.

Gross, Kenneth. *The Alice Crimmins Case.* New York: Knopf, 1975.

Hass, Robert. *Praise.* Boston: Ecco Press, 1990.

Heaney, Seamus. *District and Circle.* Boston: Farrar, Straus and Giroux, 2006.

———. *Field Work.* New York: Faber & Faber, 1979.

———. *The Government of the Tongue.* London: Faber, 1989.

———. *Poems 1965–1975.* New York: Faber & Faber, 1980.

Heyen, William. *The Rope.* Du Bois, PA: Mammoth Books, 2005.

Heyen, William. *Shoah Train.* Wilkes-Barre, PA: Etruscan Press, 2005.

———, ed. *September 11, 2001: American Writers Respond.* Wilkes-Barre, PA: Etruscan Press, 2002.

Hix, H. L. *Chromatic.* Wilkes-Barre, PA: Etruscan Press, 2006.

———. *God Bless.* Wilkes-Barre, PA: Etruscan Press, 2007.

———. *Shadows of Houses.* Wilkes-Barre, PA: Etruscan Press. 2004.

Karl, Frederick. *Joseph Conrad: The Three Lives.* New York: Farrar, Straus and Giroux, 1979.

Kelly, Brigit Pegeen. *Song.* Rochester, NY: BOA, 1995.

Kennelly, Brendan, ed. *The Penguin Book of Irish Verse.* London: Penguin, 1960.

Kessler, Milton. *The Grand Concourse.* Binghamton, NY: New Myths, 1987.

Kincaid, Jamaica. *A Small Place.* New York: Plume, 1988.

Kizer, Carolyn, trans. *Carrying Over: Poems from the Chinese, Urdu Macedonian, Yiddish, and French African.* Port Townsend, WA: Copper Canyon Press. 1988.

Knight, Etheridge. *The Essential Etheridge Knight.* Pittsburgh: University of Pittsburgh Press, 1986.

Lang, Berel, ed. *Writing and the Holocaust.* New York: Holmes & Meier, 1988.

Logan, John. *Collected Poems.* Brockport, NY: BOA Editions, 1989.

Lynch, Thomas. *Still Life in Milford.* New York: W. W. Norton & Company, 1999.

Montague, John, ed. *The Book of Irish Verse.* London: Faber, 1975.

———. *Collected Poems.* Dublin: Gallery Press, 1995.

Mullen, Jack. *Behind the Shield.* New York: Dell, 1996.

———. *In the Line of Duty.* New York: Dell, 1994.

Murray, Les. *Translations from the Natural World.* New York: Farrar, Straus and Giroux, 1992.